"Weill and Woerner's book provides a very useful framework for analyzing the best business model option and developing a transformation strategy in response to the digital revolution every company is going through."

—JAMES I. CASH JR., Lead Independent Director, Walmart

"This book will help companies to take a hard look at their digital transformation strategies and show them how to win in the fourth industrial revolution."

—FRANCISCO GONZÁLEZ, Group Executive Chairman, BBVA

"An essential decision guide to navigate digitization, ask the right questions, and make the right choices. Based on a wealth of data points and real-life examples, this book offers practical, step-by-step tips to define and execute a winning digital transformation."

—JEAN-PASCAL TRICOIRE, Chairman and CEO, Schneider Electric

"Weill and Woerner's book is a must-read primer for CEOs wondering why they need to digitally transform their companies and how to succeed in the endeavor."

—FERNANDO A. GONZÁLEZ, CEO, CEMEX

"Weill and Woerner bring laser focus to the pressing need for enterprises to digitize their business models. This book is a practical, hopeful guide for executives and boards alike, providing a call to action and a framework for execution that blends cutting-edge research with real-world examples."

—JENNIFER S. BANNER, CEO, Schaad Companies; Lead Director, BB&T

"The authors provide a simple but powerful framework for enterprises to reinvent their business models for the digital age. Their probing questions, self-assessments, and real-life examples make this book a must-read for everyone who wants to make their digital transformation a success."

—**SAMMY LEE,** Chairman and Chief Invisible Officer,
LKK Health Products Group

"A sustainable digital transformation is a journey, and the frameworks and questions outlined by Weill and Woerner provide clear and pragmatic waypoints for any executive team."

—**MAILE CARNEGIE,** Group Executive, Digital Banking, ANZ

"This important book provides a clear framework for digital transformation, including different pathways; tools for assessing what direction to take; and the skills, leadership, and culture you need to make it happen. If your goal is to stop doing 'digital lipstick' and instead to truly reinvent your digital business model, then this is a must-read!"

—**DAVID GLEDHILL,** Chief Information Officer and
Group Head Operations, DBS Bank

# WHAT'S YOUR DIGITAL BUSINESS MODEL?

PETER
WEILL

STEPHANIE L.
WOERNER

# WHAT'S YOUR DIGITAL BUSINESS MODEL?

## SIX QUESTIONS TO HELP YOU BUILD THE NEXT-GENERATION ENTERPRISE

Harvard Business Review Press

Boston, Massachusetts

10 9 8 7 6 5 4 3 2 1

The web addresses referenced in this book were live and correct at the time of the book's publication but may be subject to change.

Library of Congress Cataloging-in-Publication Data

Names: Weill, Peter, author. | Woerner, Stephanie L., author.
Title: What's your digital business model? : six questions to help you build the next-generation enterprise / by Peter D. Weill and Stephanie L. Woerner.
Description: Boston, Massachusetts : Harvard Business Review Press, [2018]
Identifiers: LCCN 2017049129 | ISBN 9781633692701 (hardcover : alk. paper)
Subjects: LCSH: Information technology—Management. | Strategic planning. | Business planning—Data processing. | Technological innovations—Management.
Classification: LCC HD30.2 W4514 2018 | DDC 658/.05—dc23 LC record available at https://lccn.loc.gov/2017049129

The paper used in this publication meets the requirements of the American National Standard for Permanence of Paper for Publications and Documents in Libraries and Archives Z39.48-1992.

ISBN: 978-1-63369-270-1
eISBN: 978-1-63369-271-8

# CONTENTS

# WHAT'S YOUR DIGITAL BUSINESS MODEL?

# Building the Next-Generation Enterprise

Digital transformation is not about technology—it's about change. And it is not a matter of *if*, but a question of when and how.

Recently, we conducted a workshop about digital disruption with the board and senior management team of a successful bank. Deep into the conversation, we were encouraging the bank to think about a new business model: to become a destination for customers navigating life events, rather than simply being a place they go to for making a transaction. People don't go to a bank looking for a mortgage, we said—they are looking to buy a home. That small shift in thinking would mean a profound shift in almost every aspect of the business, and this change was the bank's best bet for addressing the squeeze the company already felt from new digital financial services that were making a meal of its revenues.

At that point, one of the senior managers asked a serious question: "What happens if this new business model doesn't work?"

The chair of the board and the CEO, almost in unison, replied, "Then we will try something else." The CEO continued: "But we know for sure that if we don't do anything, someone else will get between us and the customer, using digital."

In the digital economy that's now upon us, many enterprises won't succeed by merely tweaking the management practices that led to past success. Larger enterprises are particular targets of digital disruption because of their large customer base, juicy profits, and sometimes-patchy customer experience. To thrive in a digitized universe, businesses of all sizes will need to reinvent themselves and substantially change their organizations, including their business models, people, structures, critical competencies, and cultures. In short, your relationship with your customers depends on creating new digital ways for them to interact with your company.

To be sure, the digital revolution is disrupting virtually every industry. In financial services, for example, customers are pulling away from long-established relationships with banks in favor of third-party apps and experiences offered by the likes of PayPal, Apple Pay, Kabbage, and Venmo. Even retailers such as Coles—the Australian supermarket chain—and the home-goods chain Ikea are claiming their share of new customer transactions, breaking into the insurance business to sell policies alongside furniture and perishables.

The numbers associated with the disruption are large indeed, and so are the ramifications. Citi estimates that global private investment in financial technology (so-called fintech) increased from US$2 billion in 2010 to US$21 billion in 2016.[1] One consequence: an estimated 30 percent of current bank-industry employees will probably lose their jobs over the next decade—and governments will have to find ways to help those people make the transition.[2] Here's another consequence: as the competition heats up, profit margins decrease and regulation increases; incumbent banks currently in the driver's seat have everything to lose. Tech firms, including fintech firms, are not as burdened by regulations as big banks are, and with mobile technologies, they have a direct link to customers.[3] If big banks don't reinvent their business models with far more compelling customer engagement, they will be caught in a cost-driven race to the bottom.

Digitization is staking claims in other industries as well. The business news is full of examples, from Uber (disrupting taxis) and Airbnb (disrupting hotels) to Amazon's disruption of retailers of all kinds—and the resulting backlash. Amazon's share of apparel sales grow daily: recently, buying behavior officially tipped away from box stores like Macy's (which in 2016 announced the closing of one hundred stores) toward Amazon, which analysts estimate will become the biggest seller of apparel in the United States by the end of 2017.[4]

In our research, we've found that digital disruption comes in three varieties:

1. **New entrants:** Startups like Uber and Airbnb—and former born-digital startups like Amazon and WeChat, which have a different business model and superior digital capabilities—enter an existing industry (often those that are complex and difficult for customers to navigate) and offer an exciting new value proposition.

2. **New business models for traditional competitors:** Existing businesses adopt a business model that is more appealing to their customers—like the challenging move Nordstrom made from a traditional department store to an attractive omnichannel business, combining the best of *place*

(tangible, product-based, customer-oriented transactions) and *space* (intangible, service based, and oriented toward the customer experience).[5] Banking, insurance, retail, and energy companies are all struggling to find that perfect mix of place and space.

3. **Crossing industry boundaries:** Enterprises that are successful in one industry (or customer domain) use digital tactics to move into a new industry or domain. We are seeing this trend in many areas like home ownership—with banks, insurance companies, realtors, and others all vying for this space.

Given the level of turmoil caused by digital disruption of all varieties, addressing it is no longer a choice; today it is a business imperative. It's time for companies to evaluate the threats, understand the opportunities, and start creating new business options for the future.

Board members at large companies agree. In our recent research at MIT's Center for Information Systems Research (http://cisr.mit.edu), board members of various companies estimated that 32 percent of their company's revenue would be under threat from digital disruption in the next five years. A full 60 percent believed that their boards should spend significantly more time on this issue next year.[6]

But how, exactly, do companies prepare for digital disruption? How do they join the ranks of digitization to take advantage of customer relationships and increase cross-selling opportunities, among other benefits? How do leaders create a compelling vision for their enterprises' success five, even ten, years from now?

Thus far, the path forward hasn't been obvious. Even though digitization is one of the biggest challenges larger enterprises have faced in a generation, and even as businesses are experimenting with new ideas every day, they often have no idea if they'll be successful. With such uncertainty, it's very hard to build a business case for digital strategy right now. Nevertheless, without a compelling vision for success in a digital economy, your enterprise will suffer a "death of a thousand cuts"—a slow and agonizing descent into a world of automation and cost competition while someone else captures the relationship with your customers.

Recent business literature describes aspects of digital disruption and offers possible solutions. But these books haven't done enough to help leaders create a winning *digital business model* (DBM). We think we know why. In our work with senior executive teams and the boards of larger companies worldwide, we discovered a surprising phenomenon: leaders lack a common language or a compelling framework to help them assess the degree of threat to their business, and—more importantly—to offer direction about what they should do.

In this book, we introduce a simple but powerful digital business model framework and language to help executives think about their competitive environments in the digital era. The framework will enable leaders to understand where they are in their digital journey, where they have to go, and which best practices will get them there. We derived the framework and material for this book by studying top financial performers and drawing on five years of field-based research, executive education, meeting and workshop facilitation, and advising. Moreover, we have studied fifty companies with in-person interviews and more than a thousand companies through survey data collected over six surveys.[7]

The result is a framework tested globally with dozens of senior management teams. The book will prove valuable to executives of larger enterprises facing both disruption and opportunity from digital. The ideas will also be valuable to startups nibbling at the best parts of big business, board members looking at the many strategic questions digital raises, and consulting firms seeking viable ideas to present to their large clients. And managers at smaller companies will also find our framework useful, as will any leader concerned with how his or her company will thrive five years from now and beyond in an increasingly digital economy.

Let's turn now to a brief introduction of the framework itself and the reasoning behind it and to an outline of the overall organization of the book.

## A Framework for Becoming a Model for Success in the Digital Economy

First, some background. For some time now, we have observed a sea change in customer needs and behavior because of changes in technology. As the bank executives in our opening example came to understand, customers today are more interested in solving life events than in buying a single item, such as a banking product. When borrowing money to buy a car, for example, a customer often wants the deal negotiated, the car delivered, and insurance and financing arranged all through a single relationship—and on a mobile device at ten o'clock at night. Customers no longer want to have to go back and forth from bank to insurance agent to car dealer to put a deal together.

Accordingly, in our research and workshops with many hundreds of enterprises, we've seen that those that successfully transform for the digital economy find ways to create a persuasive *new value proposition*—often a breakthrough in customer experience. Our framework, therefore, helps companies use digital techniques that will help them know more about their customers—be they other businesses (B2B) or the end customers themselves (B2C)—and how to solve these customers' life-event needs.

Digital transformation is not really about digital. Digital technologies—social, mobile, analytics, cloud, and the internet of things, and so forth—can create a massive change, particularly as they seem to have been developed and introduced all at once and are easily accessible to most enterprises. But the technologies are still just the vehicle. Because almost every enterprise can use these digital technologies, they don't necessarily offer a competitive advantage. The key is *differentiating your business* by offering customers something new and compelling, enabled by the vehicle that digital offers, and creating a destination customers want to visit.

We call this process *creating the next-generation enterprise.* The DBM framework we've developed is a tool for building that enterprise. Here's how it works. Our research shows that digitization is compelling companies to move their business models on two dimensions. First, they are moving from controlled value chains (à la Michael Porter circa 1980) to more-complex, networked systems.[8] Second, they are moving from less familiarity with customer needs and life events to a better, closer understanding of them, resulting in better customer engagement. Looking at these dimensions in combination results in a two-by-two framework (the DBM framework) consisting of *four distinct business models*, each within a quadrant representing different capabilities and varying average financial performance (figure I-1).

1. **Supplier:** producer that sells through other enterprises

2. **Omnichannel:** integrated value chain that creates multiproduct, multichannel customer experiences to address life events

FIGURE I-1

## Digital business model framework

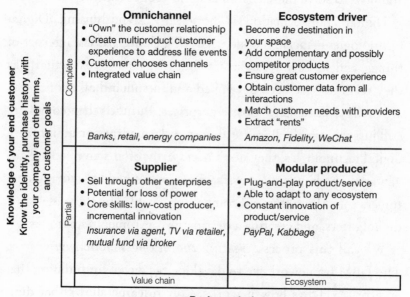

**Business design**
Who controls key decisions like brand, contracts, price,
quality, participants, IP and data ownership, regulation

*Source:* P. Weill and S. L. Woerner, "Thriving in an Increasingly Digital Ecosystem," *MIT Sloan Management Review* 56, no. 4 (June 16, 2015): 27–34. © 2017 MIT Sloan Center for Information Systems Research. Used with permission.

3. **Modular producer:** provider of plug-and-play products or services

4. **Ecosystem driver:** organizer of an ecosystem, a coordinated network of enterprises, devices, and customers to create value for all participants, which is *the* destination in a particular domain (such as shopping), ensuring great customer service; includes complementary and sometimes competitor products

To determine where a company falls in the four quadrants and where it wants to move, leaders must ask certain questions and make choices. First, they must determine to what extent they are part of a value chain that can be controlled (and that they believe they or someone must control), or to what extent they are part of a more complex digital ecosystem, in which the dynamics are less about command and control and more about building, maintaining, and using networks.

Second, executives need to assess how much they know about the needs of their end customers and how much they *can* know. Once a company has determined which quadrant or quadrants it is operating in, it can use the framework to discover whether it should stay where it is or, if not, what it should do to move toward another DBM.

There is a lot at stake in these choices. Although being part of a value chain is a perfectly manageable business model with known capabilities (such as keeping costs down and enjoying efficient supply chains)—especially in enterprises that operate B2B—for the most part, businesses operating strictly as suppliers focused narrowly on value chains could find themselves at a disadvantage. Pressure is growing, especially in companies where end customers are used to interacting digitally and expect a great experience.

On the other hand, we found that enterprises with an ecosystem-driver model had higher revenue growth and net profit margins than the other DBMs (table I-1). We believe most existing companies can build on their strong customer relationships or take advantage of their networks, assets, capital, and business partners to grow in a digital world. For example, they can increase digital cross-selling opportunities, such as what Commonwealth Bank of Australia has done with its new mobile property-valuation app to drive the sale of mortgages (more on that later in the book).[9]

In many ways, Walmart's primary business model exemplifies the value chain approach. Walmart controls everything about

TABLE I-1

## Ecosystem drivers outperform all other business models on four measures for performance

| Digital business model | Customer experience | Time to market | Revenue growth | Net profit margin |
|---|---|---|---|---|
| Supplier | 65% | 50% | 33% | 34% |
| Omnichannel | 80% | 75% | 40% | 40% |
| Modular producer | 70% | 63% | 43% | 46% |
| Ecosystem driver | 80% | 78% | 51% | 50% |

Source: MIT CISR 2013 Ecosystem Survey (101 participants) and MIT CISR-Gartner 2013 Ecosystem Survey (93 participants). Results are from companies with more than $1 billion in revenues. Self-reported net profit margin correlates to actual net profit margin at $p < 0.05$ and self-reported revenue growth correlates to actual revenue growth at $p < 0.09$. Financial measures are relative to industry. Customer experience and time to market were assessed relative to competitors. All measures were transformed to a 0–100 percent scale. Differences between models for each measure are significant at $p < 0.05$. © 2017 MIT Sloan Center for Information Systems Research. Used with permission.

its products: the price, from the supplier, where they are located in the store, and when they are sold. However, it doesn't always know who its customers are and why they are buying particular products. Digitization enables consumers and companies to know more and to seek out a wider array of benefits.

Meanwhile, the ecosystem-driver model that Amazon typifies allows greater customer choice, offers the best price available, and enables faster innovation. The enhanced consumer value comes from having different vendors selling similar (or even identical) products—often at different prices or service levels—and fast feedback, allowing vendors to improve their products and services. Consumers get a one-stop Amazon-curated experience with greater choice and with more information about prices and quality. Amazon gets to see the data on all the activity in its ecosystem while fine-tuning and identifying new opportunities and extracting rents from the merchants within the ecosystem.

Ecosystems are particularly powerful in retail. Moreover, health care (e.g., Aetna), online entertainment (e.g., Netflix), energy management (e.g., Schneider Electric), and wealth management (e.g., Fidelity) all have powerful ecosystem-driver businesses. Looking ahead, we see the trend moving toward individual and business customers preferring only one, or maybe two, powerful ecosystem drivers in each domain; the result is significant industry consolidation. This potential consolidation raises the stakes for leaders to clarify their positions and understand their options for moving toward a better DBM today.

Accordingly, some long-standing enterprises are reinventing themselves—and they view their reinvention as a journey that will continue for many years, evolving along the way. Using digital, they have some exciting visions of how they will interact with their customers. Consider these examples of such companies, both established and new:

- **Aetna—building a healthier world.** Aetna has moved from a primarily B2B health insurance enterprise to an increasingly full-service destination for customers to meet their health-care needs. From 2009 to 2014, it increased its revenue to more than three times the industry average.[10]

- **7-Eleven Japan—solving your daily needs.** 7-Eleven has moved from a chain of around 20,000 convenience stores averaging around three thousand products each, but with different selections in each store, to a single point of contact (either at the store or online) for more than three million products. 7-Eleven Japan has a 42 percent share of convenience store sales in Japan, and its profitability leads the industry average (3.4 percent vs. 1.8 percent).[11]

- **Uber—coordinating logistics through a citywide digital mesh.** Uber, the world's best-known ride-sharing enterprise, is moving into personal logistics and beyond and is growing fast.[12]

- **Schneider Electric—leading the digital transformation of energy management and automation.** Schneider Electric is moving from manufacturing and distributing thousands of electrical products to providing complete energy management and automation solutions. The company has increased its cross-selling by 20 percent.[13]

- **Amazon—creating the destination for all customer needs and more.** Amazon has moved from being an electronic bookseller to an online marketplace with more than 480 million products in the United States. The company continues to add products and services for customers and businesses.[14]

- **WeBank—reinventing banking.** WeBank is a pioneer of financially enabling social activities for the approximately eight hundred million active users on WeChat. WeBank provides banking services to enable the social activities of WeChat users—like going out to dinner, traveling, or looking for an apartment. Yet it provides these services in the background, without the user ever going to a bank or enlisting a banking app. Employing mostly data analysts, not bankers, WeBank represents a major threat to traditional banks.[15]

- **United Services Automobile Association (USAA)—solving your life events.** USAA rethought banking by moving from selling products to solving life events such as buying a car, having a child, or moving your residence. The firm regularly achieves the highest customer satisfaction scores in banking in the United States.[16]

Like these enterprises, your company can reinvent itself to compete in the digital era. In working with large enterprises around the world and across industries, we have found that the DBM framework helps executive teams address digital threats and capture opportunities to create winning strategies. But first they must ask themselves some critical questions.

## The Six Questions—and a Guide to This Book

Using the DBM framework to foster successful transformation requires that leaders first grapple with six key questions:

1. **Threat:** How strong is the digital threat to your business model?

2. **Model:** Which business model is best for your enterprise's future?

3. **Advantage:** What is your competitive advantage?

4. **Connection:** How will you use mobile technologies and the internet of things (IoT) to connect and learn?

5. **Capabilities:** Are you buying options for the future and preparing for the necessary organizational surgery?

6. **Leadership:** Do you have the leadership at all levels to make transformation happen?

Most enterprises don't get their transformations right the first time, and iteration is as critical as vision and inspiration. And perhaps that's the most important lesson of all. It's very rare—in fact, we can't remember any examples—to see an enterprise create a great vision and plan for transformation and implement it without significant course corrections. Enterprises need to answer, with actionable decisions, the six questions we've just listed and then iterate, course-correct, and learn from their actions to go to the next step in the continuous journey of reinvention. It's this willingness and flexibility that we think differentiates success from failure.

This book will lead you through each of the six questions—one question per chapter. Each chapter provides a structure to help you answer the question, an assessment to help you figure out where you are, data on what top-performing enterprises do, and motivating case studies of enterprises that have excelled. By the end of each chapter, you should be able to decide what action to take (figure I-2). Examples and cases cited throughout the book include Aetna, Amazon, BBVA, Commonwealth Bank of Australia, DBS Bank, Dunkin' Donuts, Fidelity, Garanti Bank, Johnson & Johnson, PayPal, Procter & Gamble, Schindler, Schneider Electric, 7-Eleven Japan, USAA, and Woolworths.

In chapter 1 we examine the various threats and opportunities enterprises are facing from digitization. We use case studies to inspire and share what has worked in other businesses grappling with similar issues. The key action here is to *identify the level of threat* your enterprise now faces. We'll finish the chapter with a self-assessment to help you do that.

Chapter 2 focuses on the DBM framework that we described earlier in this introduction, that is, the four possible business models in a digital economy: ecosystem driver, omnichannel, modular producer, and supplier. We describe a leading enterprise in each

FIGURE I-2

## Six key questions and actions for transformation in the digital economy

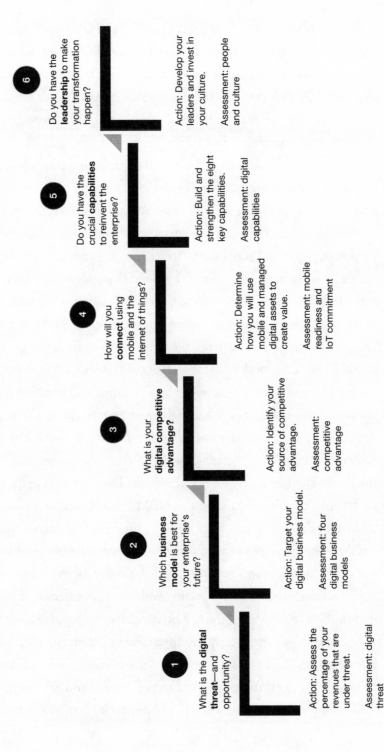

**1** What is the **digital threat**—and opportunity?

Action: Assess the percentage of your revenues that are under threat.

Assessment: digital threat

**2** Which **business model** is best for your enterprise's future?

Action: Target your digital business model.

Assessment: four digital business models

**3** What is your **digital competitive advantage?**

Action: Identify your source of competitive advantage.

Assessment: competitive advantage

**4** How will you **connect** using mobile and the internet of things?

Action: Determine how you will use mobile and managed digital assets to create value.

Assessment: mobile readiness and IoT commitment

**5** Do you have the crucial **capabilities** to reinvent the enterprise?

Action: Build and strengthen the eight key capabilities.

Assessment: digital capabilities

**6** Do you have the **leadership** to make your transformation happen?

Action: Develop your leaders and invest in your culture.

Assessment: people and culture

model—Aetna, PayPal, Procter & Gamble, and USAA—and show how enterprises are changing models over time. And we show which models have the best growth, net profit margins, customer experience, and levels of innovation. Specifically, we explore the two dimensions of major change enabled by digitization: getting closer to end customers and moving from supplier models (value chains like the traditional Walmart) to digital ecosystems (such as Amazon). Enterprises that are both closer to their end customers and earn most of their revenues from ecosystems have, up to now, outperformed their industry-average profitability by more than 25 percent. But the ecosystem-driver model is hard to get right. Other models may not offer the financial performance that the ecosystem driver currently does, but other business outcomes can be as important as profitability, in the short term. And not every enterprise will be able to make the move to ecosystem driver right away. There are good intermediary goals to shoot for—such as opening up the company to more partnerships and learning more about the end customers. This chapter primarily aims to help you determine *which business model in the DBM framework is best for your enterprise* to create a new, compelling customer offer. We finish the chapter with a self-assessment. The first part helps you find your current position in the DBM framework, and the second part asks where you want to be in the next five years.

Chapter 3 describes how to *identify and capitalize on your main sources of competitive advantage.* In a digital economy with many new competitors, senior executives have to understand what makes their enterprises great. Enterprises can compete digitally with one or more of three capabilities: their content (products and information), their customer experience (multichannel and multiproduct), and their digitized platforms (internal and external). We explore the issues with case studies of digital leaders like Amazon,

BBVA, Commonwealth Bank of Australia, LexisNexis, TripAd-visor, USAA, and Wall Street Journal. Using results from our effective-practices survey, we describe how the top-performing enterprises identify and exploit their competitive advantage. We finish the chapter with a self-assessment exercise to help you iden-tify the most important sources of competitive advantage for your enterprise's future success—and discuss next steps.

Chapter 4 explores the importance of connectivity to success in the next-generation enterprise. Connectivity is the essence of digitization and is enabling new business models every day. We illustrate connectivity with the promise of the IoT and mobile—a connected world leading to new ways to delight customers and make money. Together mobile and the IoT will change almost everything. Estimates of the IoT business market are as high as US$19 trillion; such projections have led to lots of lofty talk and strategic positioning.[17] However, our research indicates that while there is great opportunity, top- and bottom-line value is typi-cally created only by enterprises willing to make the hard choices necessary to change their business models. We illustrate how to achieve connectivity with case studies of Dunkin' Donuts, Flex, GE, iGaranti, Johnson & Johnson, and Schindler. In this chapter, we ask the following question: *How will you use mobile and dig-itally managed assets to connect and create value?*

In chapter 5, we argue that enterprises will not succeed in the digital economy merely by tweaking the management prac-tices that led to past success. To thrive, many enterprises will need to make investments in structures, skills, and practices to substantially change their organization. We discuss two key ac-tions companies can take. They can build a digital culture and structure—the shared values, beliefs, traditions, and assump-tions about digital—that guide behaviors. And they can become ambidextrous by simultaneously innovating and cutting costs. We return to the DBM framework and identify the eight organizational capabilities necessary for the next-generation enterprise:

- Gathering great information about customers (e.g., their goals)

- Amplifying the customer voice inside the enterprise (making the customer central to everything the enterprise does)

- Creating a culture of evidence-based decision making (using customer, operational, market, and social data)

- Providing an integrated, multiproduct, multichannel customer experience

- Being distinctive, and becoming the first place your best customers think of when a need arises

- Identifying and developing great partnerships and acquisitions

- Service-enabling your core business capabilities (implementing business capabilities in reusable modular software components) and making them available using application programming interface (APIs)

- Developing efficiency, compliance, and security as enterprise competencies

We describe how several enterprises, including Aetna and BBVA, are creating digital cultures and reinventing their next-generation enterprises to win in the digital economy. The self-assessment in this chapter helps you determine how good you are at the eight organizational capabilities and where you need to focus.

Chapter 6, our final chapter, discusses a key role of leaders in creating the next-generation enterprise: *identifying and leveraging leaders throughout the organization to enact the needed changes.* Transformation requires leadership from all parts of the organization—top down and bottom up. We talk about the roles of the important players: the board, the CEO, the executive committee, the chief information officer (CIO), and the workforce, including middle management and younger employees. We illustrate the leadership challenges with insights from DBS Bank, Deloitte, ING, and Microsoft; provide an assessment to help you identify gaps in your leadership; and recommend how to begin leading the transformation to the next-generation enterprise.

Right now is both an exciting and a daunting time to be a leader of a large enterprise. The stakes are very high. Digital disruption is already here, and doing nothing will lead to the aforementioned slow death of a thousand cuts. The goal of this book is to provide a common language, helpful frameworks, motivating case studies, and data on early financial performance to help you reach the difficult decisions you must make to set up their enterprises for success in the next decades.

Let's get started.

# What Is the Digital Threat—and Opportunity?

By 2013 BBVA's Francisco González, executive chairman of the global bank headquartered in Spain, had been worried for some time. BBVA needed to act increasingly swiftly and decisively to meet changing customer behavior. Banking was facing imminent digital disruption, and González feared that customers would start to take up less of BBVA's services in favor of more innovative financial services offered by internet startups and the internet giants—the so-called "over-the-top" players.

He had good reason to fear. A 2013 survey of the global banking industry found that customer loyalty was diminishing; customers were making decisions quicker and accessing financial offerings from firms that weren't traditional banks.[1] More than 70 percent of retail banking customers surveyed in North America in 2014 considered their banking relationship to be mostly transactional, and more than 25 percent said they would consider managing their money with a bank with no branch locations. In addition, customers wanted more proactive advice and real-time analysis of their spending habits.[2] As González told us at the time, "There is a rapidly growing gap between customer behavior and retail banks."[3]

Clearly BBVA had to figure out a response to these threats. González knew that if it were done well, a solution would mean enormous opportunity for BBVA and the bank's own digital future. But before he could devise a response, he first had to understand how big, exactly, the threat was. What part and how much of the enterprise was under siege from digitization?

We will return shortly to BBVA's story and how its leaders answered that question. For now we'll say that, like González, every leader needs first to determine the level of threat presented by digitization. Only then will the opportunities become apparent.

In this chapter, we'll point you to a self-assessment to help you see how much threat your company is facing from digital disruption, and we'll look at enterprises that have examined their own threat levels. Finally, we will describe the kinds of opportunities that companies such as BBVA, Dunkin' Donuts, and others have explored in pursuit of digitization.

## How Big Is the Threat?

To learn how urgently you must act, how radical the organizational surgery should be, and what opportunities lie ahead, start by doing the chapter 1 self-assessment. Give a numerical score to the likelihood of your best-selling product or service being digitally disrupted. Next, using that score and the importance of your best-seller in your business, estimate the percentage of your enterprise's revenues under threat from digital disruption over the next five years. Then, compare your response with figure 1-1, which depicts 413 senior executives' responses to our survey. (For one enterprise's story of identifying the level of digital threat to its business, see the sidebar "Digital Threats and Opportunities at Schneider Electric.")

---

**CHAPTER 1**

## Self-assessment

**A. What is the impact of digitization on your enterprise?**

*Think of your best-selling product or service. On a scale from **0** (low) to **20** (high), score each question.*

To what extent is this product or service:

1. Electronically specifiable and searchable? ☐

2. Either is—or is going to be—delivered digitally in the next five years? ☐

3. Augmented (or can be augmented) with valuable information? ☐

4. Threatened by enterprises in other industries—that have relationships with your customers—offering competitive services to yours and disrupting your business? ☐

5. At risk of being replaced with an alternative digital offering (e.g., books, classroom education, medical diagnosis, 3-D printing)? ☐

**Total** ☐

Scores of 70 and higher indicate that your best-selling product or service is at great risk of being digitally disrupted.

**B. Based on your score (from A), estimate the percentage of your company's revenues that are under threat from digital disruption over the next five years (e.g., new technology-based models disrupting successful businesses).** ☐

*Source:* MIT CISR.

---

**FIGURE 1-1**

## Senior executive survey: revenues threatened by digital disruption

*Total average revenues under threat:* **28 percent**. *Average revenues under threat in large firms (greater than $7 billion in annual revenues):* **46 percent**.

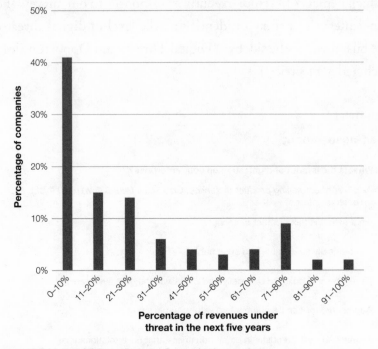

**Percentage of revenues under threat in the next five years**

*Source:* MIT CISR 2015 CIO Digital Disruption Survey of 413 respondents.

Figure 1-1 tells an interesting story. The average senior executive expects that 28 percent of his or her enterprise's revenue will be under threat from digital disruption over the next five years. That is, the enterprise will lose this revenue if it does nothing different. Therefore, prudent senior executive teams must plan how to defend or replace almost a third of the enterprise's revenue in the next five years—no small feat. They do this by making significant investments in new areas to protect the business—buying options for the future—which we'll explore in detail later. But not all enterprises are affected equally.

Both the size and the industry of each of those enterprises make a difference. Large enterprises with more than US$7 billion in revenues have the most to lose—their executives estimate that an average of 46 percent of their revenues is under threat. Large enterprises are threatened usually because of their hefty profits and their inability to change rapidly—providing a perfect slow-moving target for an outside digital disrupter to pursue.

Some industries, like media, face more threat from digitization than others do. ESPN, for example, offers a cautionary tale of what can happen if you don't figure out how you will be disrupted. In 2011, ESPN's future looked assured. With a hundred million subscribers, and offered as part of almost every cable package, the network helped its parent, Disney, record strong profits. Five years later, however, profits were shrinking, the subscriber base—especially young people—was leaving, and the cost of programming had increased (ESPN has been an aggressive bidder for games). Game highlights, an ESPN programming mainstay, are readily available on social media. As a result, ESPN has begun monitoring social media to learn which sports stories are trending. It is also refashioning some of its shows and is providing a user interface that allows viewers to see all the offerings on all its channels. Rather than re-create itself, ESPN is trying to protect its business model by improving the customer experience.[4]

Time will tell whether ESPN's strategy will work or will result in a death of a thousand cuts. Later in the book, we will talk about the impact of the IoT on the manufacturing sector, where we are beginning to see that enterprises with new connected business models are performing significantly better than their rivals are.

## Digital Threats and Opportunities at Schneider Electric

Schneider Electric provides a good illustration of one company's journey toward digital transformation—and becoming a next-generation enterprise.[a] Founded in France in 1836 as a producer of steel and expanding into heavy machine and transportation equipment soon thereafter, Schneider Electric has evolved to become a global leader in energy management and automation. It operates in four markets: building and partner (43 percent of revenues), infrastructure (20 percent), industry (22 percent), and IT (15 percent).

Between 2002 and 2008, Schneider Electric doubled in size, from both organic growth and acquisitions.[b] This growth, however, along with a history of business-unit autonomy, created a lot of variability and fragmentation of enterprise processes, resulting in cost inefficiencies and missed revenue opportunities. Customers and employees were sometimes frustrated by the complexity.

By 2008, Schneider Electric's leaders began to consider the digital threat to the company's business model and the opportunity that could stem from the ability to offer end-to-end digital solutions to its customers. They knew they had to address the company's complexity to simplify the customer experience and to proactively deal with the disruption that digitization posed to its business model. The potential disruption came in many forms. For example, other large companies wanted to be the destination for their current customers and selling many of the products Schneider Electric currently sold. Smaller, more local companies could provide similar products to Schneider Electric's, perhaps at a lower price, and customers could find them through a digital search. More-connected systems could be managed by companies other than Schneider Electric. Add a myriad of startups with a bewildering array of new technologies trying to bite into Schneider Electric's market share, and the level of potential digital disruption was high indeed. This was the starting point from which Schneider Electric could begin to understand its current business model and identify next steps to lead the company toward a more desirable model.

a. The information on the history and transformation of Schneider Electric comes from our interviews and conversations with senior Schneider Electric executives, particularly CIO Hervé Coureil and CEO Jean-Pascal Tricoire; our presentation at a digital strategy retreat in Hong Kong in 2011; N. Fonstad and J. Ross, "Building Business Agility: Cloud-Based Services and Digitized Platform Maturity," *Massachusetts Institute of Technology, Sloan School of Management, Center for Information Systems Research (MIT CISR) Briefing* 15, no. 2 (February 2015); A. Karunakaran, J. Mooney, and J. W. Ross, "Accelerating Global Digital Platform Deployment Using the Cloud: A Case Study of Schneider Electric's 'Bridge Front Office' Program," working paper 399 MIT CISR, Cambridge, MA, January 2015); S. Scantlebury "Redesigning Schneider Electric's Operating Model," case vignette, MIT CISR, Cambridge, MA 2015; and Schneider Electric, "Mobile and Tablet Applications," *Life Is On* (Schneider Electric blog), accessed October 22, 2017, www.schneider-electric.co.uk/en/work/support/apps.

b. Schneider Electric 2009 Annual Report. Within six years, Schneider Electric doubled in size through organic growth and by making nearly fifteen acquisitions each year. Revenue jumped from EUR 9 billion in 2002 to EUR 18.3 billion in 2008, reflecting annual average growth of 12 percent.

Add robotics and other kinds of automation, and these industries will change dramatically.

Returning to the case of BBVA, Francisco González evaluated the threat—and indeed opportunity—digital posed for the financial services industry as very high: "Some bankers and analysts think that Google, Facebook, Amazon, or the like will not fully enter a highly regulated, low-margin business such as banking. I disagree. What is more, I think banks that are not prepared for such new competitors face certain death."[5] González continued: "Most banks look only at the rooftop—the products and services that customers see. The problem is if you only build the rooftop, and don't change the structure underneath, the whole building becomes very unstable."[6]

One step that BBVA took in order to prepare for the future was to invest in Garanti Bank, Turkey's second-largest private bank. Garanti has been a pioneer in digital banking, especially in mobile banking. González said, "Garanti operates in a market that has great growth potential and has a similar business model to that of BBVA, which is customer-centric and technology-based."[7]

## What Opportunities Await Your Company?

The kind of threat level that González determined BBVA was facing in 2013 leaves banks at a fork in the road, squarely in front of two diverging paths. One route is to specialize in handling the back end of the banking transaction and let other enterprises handle the customer-centric front end (such as PayPal's offering payment services to many customer-facing businesses). In fact, in the short to medium term, some banks will probably operate the highly regulated back end of financial transactions like payments, but there will be fewer of those banks. Because these sorts of transactions are a commodity play and a race to the bottom in terms of margins, they amount to a very operational and industrialized business.

A more promising route is to get out in front of digitization and discover how to meet customer needs with an integrated omnichannel (as described in figure I-1 in the introduction) that includes engaging, even fun, services. Banks need to think more about cannibalizing their own traditional products, using their detailed customer and product data to determine what customers want and to become a place that customers can rely on to solve life-event challenges such as buying a car or house. This change will typically require some organizational surgery to exploit the digital opportunity that comes from shifting from a product focus to putting customers first.

For example, Garanti (of which BBVA is the leading share-holder) decided that to successfully target new, young customers, the bank needed to do something other than relying solely on its thousand branches to provide services. Consequently, iGaranti was born. This mobile app, a smart financial coach, addresses the everyday financial needs of millennials and removes the need to walk into a branch.[8] Today, iGaranti has more than 4.1 million active mobile customers.[9]

But for most banks—as yet unproven in meeting customers' life-event needs—the idea of giving up back-end transaction processing such as payments is too radical a change. We expect that those banks will attempt to travel down both roads simul-taneously, an effort likely to make the digitization journey even harder. Why? Efficiency in back-end processing requires a focus on standardization, automation, and reuse, while improving the customer experience entails integration of products and services to create customized solutions, a focus on the user, and numerous flexible ways for customers to interact with the bank. These two paths require different skill sets and different ways of organizing and governing the enterprise.

Ultimately, however, seizing digital opportunities will require banks to move to a new model and become low-cost, highly regulated, and industrialized financial-transaction processors. At the same time, they'll need to reinvent their customer experience to delight customers and make banks the first point of call rather than allowing the customer's retailer, mortgage or insurance broker, tech provider, or telco to take on that role.

At BBVA, in response to the threat level hovering around banking, González articulated the future that the bank intended to seize: "We think we have a huge opportunity to become the first bank in the world to successfully transform into a pure digital house. It's not just about being a bank; it's about being a knowledge-based information company."[10] In 2015 he simplified the vision to say, "We are building the best digital bank of the 21st century."[11]

Fortunately, BBVA had already laid a lot of the groundwork. It had always been a tech-savvy bank, investing heavily in reusable global platforms from 2007 onward to compete in more than thirty countries serving seventy-one million customers. Moreover, it worked hard at removing the tangled set of partly digitized business processes that had built up over time with many systems and versions of the data. At the same time, it started to replace those old processes and systems with more efficient and scalable global digital platforms. Those platforms were designed to combine optimized business processes, efficient technology, and accessible data—all at a lower cost than incurred by industry competitors, while meeting all regulatory needs. New cloud technologies pose a new challenge that finds BBVA in a privileged position to leverage from the learnings and achievements of this recent transformation.

To respond to the digital challenge, in 2014 the company appointed Carlos Torres Vila as head of a new digital banking unit. This unit worked hard to deploy digital tools, such as apps and interactive ATMs, allowing customers to do more self-service and providing the same level of service across all channels. Processes were targeted for further automation. Branches were redesigned with a thought toward improving customer experience. The efforts were successful. Digital engagement of customers increased significantly, and customer satisfaction improved, as did crossselling and cost to serve. Most important, the new digital initiatives proved the digital concept to the board, illustrating that it was possible and desirable to make the entire bank digital.

Then, in 2015, BBVA announced radical organizational surgery to move the bank another step closer to González's vision of a digital bank. Carlos Torres Vila was named CEO, and the bank was reorganized to smooth the move to digital. The new structure created five new organizational groups: execution and performance (a group that includes country networks as well as corporate and investment banking), risk and finance, business development (in 2016 it was integrated within customer solutions), strategy and control, and a group focused on new core competencies. The core competencies, which provided shared world-class core banking services, included:

- **Talent and culture:** promoting new schemes for talent management and adapting BBVA's culture to the new digital context

- **Customer and client solutions:** delivering the best banking experience to customers across all channels, and leveraging data and design to better meet customer expectations

- **Global marketing and digital sales:** driving sales across digital channels, and promoting global marketing initiatives. (In 2016, this unit was integrated within customer solutions.)

- **Engineering:** responsible for technological infrastructures, architecture, and security as well as ensuring reliability and business enablement across all software development and banking operation processes

- **New digital businesses unit:** developing new digital businesses and fostering cooperation with startups and other participants in the innovation ecosystem, such as universities and incubators. (In 2016, this unit was integrated within customer solutions.)

The business groups for execution and performance, new core competencies, risk and finance, and initially business development reported to Torres Vila, while González oversaw the newly formed strategy and control group. This new structure aimed to move BBVA from a more traditional brick-and-mortar bank with good digital capability to a fully integrated omnichannel bank with world-class banking services. The structure was designed to take advantage of digital by creating the best modular banking services that could be locally customized to meet customer needs while ensuring an efficient engineering operation with regulatory compliance. The new structure also placed BBVA's talent where it could have most impact.

As a result, today the local country networks focus on what's different in each country and on growing the local businesses. The core capability and business development teams focus on creating the best banking services possible and making them available to customers.

The new digital business unit's mandate was to experiment, to keep the bank fresh, and to limit further disruptions down the road. Besides making acquisitions—such as Simple (a US online banking startup for B2C customers) and Holvi (a Finnish online business banking service)—or creating internal ventures to build a portfolio of digital businesses that may compete with BBVA, this unit is also creating partnerships to explore new solutions.

This is a bold, strategic initiative by BBVA based on the vision of Francisco González. It's too early to tell how successful it will be and what other kinds of changes BBVA will need to make over the next decade. But the early indicators are very positive: BBVA is number one or two in customer experience among peer banks in most of its largest country operations, and the bank generated about 25 percent of its sales digitally in 2017.[12] The transformation is in full swing.

Whatever the outcome of BBVA's new vision and organizational surgery, virtually all large enterprises will need to create their own version of a compelling vision and the next-generation enterprise. And then they must implement a series of steps that will lead to the kind of transformation we are seeing at BBVA.

Although financial services like BBVA perhaps face the most critical challenge of all industries today, it's only a matter of time before most of the world's industries will have to reckon with similar tasks.

## Dunkin' Brands

For some industries and companies, however, digital creates more opportunity than threat. Take the case of Dunkin' Brands, a leading franchisor of quick-service restaurants, with more than nineteen thousand restaurants in nearly sixty countries and two major brands: Dunkin' Donuts and Baskin-Robbins ice cream. Dunkin' Donuts sells quintessentially physical products—hot coffee and a myriad of tempting doughnuts and other baked goods—which will not be digitally disrupted (at least not in the foreseeable future). It's a successful enterprise, with a 2016 net profit margin of 22.9 percent (compared with an industry average of 9.7 percent) on total store revenues of US$10.8 billion.[13] Dunkin' Brands has a 100 percent franchised business model, and up until recently, there was little direct connection between the Dunkin' Brands headquarters and the end customer.

But all that is changing. Digital mobile technology offers enormous opportunities, for the first time, to interact with the end customer, a boon for franchisors that typically know very little about the people who buy their goods and services (as opposed to the franchisees). Dunkin' Brands leaders realized that while digitization posed some threat—competitors might use digital to disrupt customer habits, or large franchisees might use the technologies to consolidate the customer relationship—on the whole, there was much more opportunity. The company identified three major areas to pursue:

- **Develop a single source of truth about end customers:** For franchisors like Dunkin' Brands, it's very difficult to get accurate, up-to-date information about end customers. Franchise restaurant operators vary in their diligence, capabilities, and motivation in collecting end-customer data, making it difficult for Dunkin' Brands to get a global view.

- **Engage customers via an omnichannel model:** As described earlier, one successful destination for companies to aim for is the upper left quadrant of the DBM framework: the omnichannel model. In this model, companies focus on providing their customers with a rich experience on and across channels. Given that virtually all Dunkin' Donuts customers today carry a mobile device, the company can, for the first time in history, implement an effective omni-channel model to engage end customers more deeply.

- **Create a loyalty program with mobile payments:** Loyalty programs and credit-card purchases for relatively small amounts, such as the average amount on a customer receipt at a Dunkin' Donuts store, have always been difficult for franchise restaurant operators, given the equipment needed and the credit-card fees. Prepaid cards, stored-value loyalty cards, and other similar models can make these payments relatively easy and less costly while implementing a cross-network loyalty program.

To capture these opportunities, in August 2012 Dunkin' Donuts launched its first mobile app, which included the ability to pay using the app. This was an opportunity to create a deep relationship with the end customers. The company's rewards program, DD Perks, introduced in 2014, offered targeted promotions and incentives to end customers, further driving the app's adoption. With more than eighteen million downloads by the first half of 2017, the app (including DD Perks' 6.6 million members) has cut seconds off service speed, increased cross-selling, enabled easy payments, and raised the average size of the order. In 2016, almost $500 million in sales was made on mobile devices (mobile payments have grown by nearly 70 percent since 2015). DD Perks members made up more than 10 percent of store transactions in the fourth quarter of 2016.

The app and the overall digital strategy create a win-win-win for Dunkin' Brands, its franchisees, and its customers. This strategy provides a rare opportunity for franchise owners to connect directly with customers and build loyalty across the network of franchise operators who are often independent small businesses. What's more, Dunkin' Brands can effectively use the data collected to improve services—and to test different strategies in different markets and learn from them. To be sure, today we are witnessing the early stages of digital transformation of retailers of physical goods, particularly of highly perishable products like the pastries, sandwiches, and coffee offered by Dunkin' Donuts. And given the benefits to franchise owners to create a deeper connection with end customers, continued experimentation across these vast networks will no doubt yield more digital innovation to come for these types of business models.

---

Before we move to the next chapter, consider again the self-assessment you did at the beginning of this chapter. How much of your business is under threat by digitization? If your business doesn't face substantial threat, can you identify opportunities that digitization offers, like the possibility of a deeper connection to your customers? Identifying the threats and potential opportunities is just the first step. In the next chapter, we'll examine the DBM framework in detail and help you determine which of the four business models is best for your enterprise to create compelling new offerings for customers.

**CHAPTER 2**

# Which Digital Business Model Is Best for Your Future?

What makes your enterprise great? And how can digitization convert that greatness into top performance? Those are key questions for businesses wishing to remain viable five years from today and beyond.

Consider a simple example—TripAdvisor, a company that gathers advice online on travel choices and planning, including more than half a billion traveler reviews of a variety of global attractions, accommodations, and restaurants. It leveraged what it did best (advice and reviews) by tapping Google's mapping service through an application programming interface (API). So today, if you're in Burgos, Spain, and looking for the perfect restaurant that's within walking distance from your hotel in the medieval city, TripAdvisor offers recommendations—and directions through the cobbled streets to get you there. By combining its user-tested travel advice with a digitized service that provides maps (as well as links to the company's many other offerings such as hotel bookings), TripAdvisor grew to become the world's largest travel site, reaching 455 million average unique monthly visitors in forty-nine markets worldwide.[1]

Why do customers repeatedly return to TripAdvisor? The site allows them to transact in a digital business ecosystem; such a coordinated network of enterprises, devices, and customers creates value for all the participants. The activities of a business ecosystem include search, information delivery, payments, and other exchanges enabled by digital connections. Ecosystems broaden what makes you great as an enterprise by adding complementary products and making them available through digital services.[2]

As described earlier, such companies, or ecosystem drivers, sit in the upper right quadrant of our digital business-model framework (DBM framework) shown in figure I-1 of the introduction. We will examine all four quadrants in depth in this chapter. Customers of all kinds, whether they are B2B or B2C, will increasingly prefer the efficiency of a go-to digital ecosystem driver to conduct transactions in every domain of living, from health care and shopping to entertainment, finance, business information, and more. Yet only 12 percent of large enterprises (including Amazon, Fidelity, and WeChat) currently earn most of their revenues from this model.[3]

Clearly this gap between what consumers want and what's available to them represents a tremendous opportunity for businesses—especially smaller enterprises, which are seizing the digital-disruption opportunity faster than their larger counterparts are (more on that dynamic later in this chapter). There is no time to waste, since several first-mover advantages—such as the brand recognition of becoming the leading destination in a domain—await enterprises that make the transition sooner rather than later.

Amazon has parlayed a strong first-mover advantage into a dominant industry position. One of the big breakthroughs of digitization—search—helped bolster Amazon's position. Search (and the associated data) changes everything; it makes the location and prices of products and services more easily found and transparent to customers. Search, and better data on customers, is part of what makes Amazon a key ecosystem driver and Walmart, historically at least, a quintessential example of what we call omnichannel in our framework. That is, Walmart has traditionally acted as a value chain as described by Michael Porter in the 1980s—engaged in episodic, often disconnected transactions in which products move from a "supplier" to the store to the customer.

Search also helps an enterprise sustain its position in a particular business model. Customers search using what they know (and enhanced brand recognition makes that brand one of the first to be entered into the search box). For example, in 2015, Amazon accounted for 44 percent of all customer searches for products in the United States. The next 24 percent of searches went to search engines like Bing and Google. The next 10 percent went directly to brands that people were searching for, such as Hitachi or Fidelity. To illustrate the power of an ecosystem driver's potential first-mover advantage, Amazon's share of searches for consumer products rose to 55 percent by late 2016.[4]

The kind of dominant position Amazon has achieved in its retail ecosystem is hard to beat. But now Walmart, acknowledging that it has fallen behind Amazon in attracting digital customers, is trying to play catch-up by significantly increasing its investment in e-commerce.[5] Recently, one of us (PW) ordered some barbecue coals on Amazon, not looking carefully at who the seller was. The coals arrived a few days later in a box from Walmart.com. That's the power of a great ecosystem. And it offers insight into how Walmart is both competing against Amazon and partnering with it by providing the coals as a modular producer to Amazon's ecosystem driver model. It will be interesting to watch Walmart play catch-up given Amazon's success.

In chapter 1, you evaluated the threat level and considered the opportunities that digitization represents to your enterprise. Now you're ready to determine exactly where your company stands today and where you'd like to be in the future, with a goal of getting closer to your customer and improving revenues by becoming more connected.

We'll begin here with a self-assessment to help you determine your current place in our DBM framework. Then we'll examine the framework and its origins in more detail, followed by examples of how to move a business up and to the right on the framework—where the most profitable businesses are. We'll conclude with some thoughts on how to clarify which quadrant in the DBM framework you think your enterprise should aim for.

## What's Your Model?

Our study of digital disruption showed us firsthand the wisdom of science fiction writer William Gibson's observation that "the future is already here—it's just not evenly distributed."[6] To determine how much of the future world of digitization your business currently operates in, take a moment to fill in the chapter 2 assessment, part 1. Then pinpoint which model your enterprise currently reflects in our DBM framework, using the chapter 2 assessment, part 2. Is your enterprise a supplier? An omnichannel? A modular producer? An ecosystem driver?

CHAPTER 2

## Self-assessment, part 1

### A. Knowledge of your end customer

Consider your best-selling product or service category.

Please use a scale from **1** (Not at all) **to 7** (Completely)

**To what extent does your enterprise know:**

- The identity of the most important end customers of your products or services?

- Their purchase history with your enterprise?

- Their purchase history with your competitors?

- Their purchase history of all products your enterprise sells?

- Their interaction history with your enterprise?

- Their business goals (for B2B) or personal goals (for B2C)?

- Their purchase decision-making process?

**Subtotal**

**Double your subtotal, then add 2.** (Maximum score: 100)

### B. Business design

A *value chain* is organized around a dominant enterprise's products and services (like the production and sale of a single company's bottled drinks). An *ecosystem* is organized to enhance the end customers' experience in a broad domain and is created with a network of partners, suppliers, complementors, and other customers.

For all your products and services, estimate the percentage of your previous year's revenues that were from ecosystems you participate in.

**Percent of revenues from ecosystems now**

*Now see part 2 of this assessment to identify your current position.*

*Source:* © 2017 MIT Sloan Center for Information Systems Research. Used with permission.

CHAPTER 2

## Self-assessment, part 2

*Mark your current position using your scores from part 1 of the assessment. The maximum scores on both the vertical axis and the horizontal axis are 100, with scores of 50 sitting above (or to the right of) the crosshairs and 50 or less below (or to the left).*

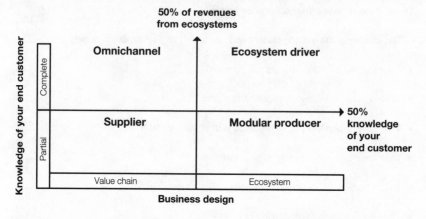

*Source:* © 2017 MIT Sloan Center for Information Systems Research. Used with permission.

Most large enterprises will operate in *more than one of these models.* The presence of more than one model isn't undesirable as long as there are synergies or good reasons to diversify. For example, not only is Amazon an ecosystem driver, but it also provides many services to other businesses, some of which Amazon also uses, including fulfillment, payment, and technology capability (through its Amazon Web Services), making it a modular producer as well. As part of its fulfillment service, Amazon handles the warehousing, packing, and shipping of one billion items. (The fulfillment service has grown quickly, with the number of sellers using the service increasing more than 70 percent in 2016, 50 percent in 2015, and 65 percent in 2014, with particularly strong growth in international sales.[7])

Most banks, too, typically operate in several quadrants—often all four and often at significantly different profit margins. For example, the typical large bank will act as a supplier, selling mortgages, investment products, and other services through financial advisers. Most banks also work hard to improve their omnichannel offerings, often by reimagining the branch to be more of a customer acquisition, sales, and advisory location with most transactions done digitally—more and more on mobile devices. These same banks operate as modular producers offering various services, including payments and foreign exchange to many other enterprises, using automated platforms. And finally, many banks have made forays into the ecosystem-driver model, often by offering more complete services for life events such as buying a house, owning a car, or preparing for retirement.

When determining which quadrant your enterprise currently calls home, ask yourself, How does the business engage customers? Does it engage them in the same way that most physical retailers do—companies that often don't know who their customers are and what they've bought before or elsewhere? Or are your interactions more like Amazon's: continuous, collaborative engagements with customers, enhanced with knowledge of their purchase and search habits? In such a well-functioning ecosystem, the customer often doesn't realize, or need to know, which enterprise is actually proving the product or service. The customer relies on the Amazon ecosystem and its brand promise to manage all that.

How does Amazon do it? The online retailer collects deep knowledge of its end customers. This capability will be critical to your own enterprise as it moves up and to the right on the DBM framework. Deep knowledge includes knowing customer names and addresses, demographics, internet protocol (IP) addresses, purchase histories with your enterprise and with other enterprises, and, most important, their life events like buying a house or having a child or business events like a merger or the opening of a branch in a new location. Such knowledge enables your enterprise to make more attractive offers and increase customer engagement—a prime goal for any enterprise.

For example, when the Commonwealth Bank of Australia (CBA) thought critically about its mortgage business, it realized that a customer's personal goal is not to get a mortgage—it's to buy a house. So CBA created a smartphone app that initially allowed users to point their phone at a house of interest to review its sale price history and those of the houses nearby. Prospective home buyers become more informed about house prices in their target areas and—if the users set up a profile they also become a hot source of mortgage leads for CBA. In-app calculators help customers assess how much they can borrow, their repayment terms, and what their up-front costs are. Users can save their calculations and complete a conditional eligibility application.[8] Applying for a mortgage was later added as a service on the app. Happily for CBA, the mortgage acquirer becomes a long-term customer of the bank—the best kind of customer. The mobile app now combines housing locations with information about the actual selling prices of the property, closing dates, estimated current values, and fast tracking of the mortgage offer. Customers have made more than 1.2 million property searches to date, and CBA estimates the app's return on investment is 109 percent.[9]

Like CBA, you need to think about how deeply you know your customers and how to gather and use more of that knowledge. These elements will help your enterprise move to a more viable model.

## Understanding the Four Business Models

When we first started researching digitization in March 2012, we began by asking senior executives to describe their enterprises' most important digitally enabled transformation initiatives to achieve breakthrough performance. We collected 144 initiatives that included everything from new architecture and platforms to better support for process automation and channel integration, to full real-time integration of external partners, to a multichannel approach to improve customer experience, efficiency, and rate of growth.[10]

When we distilled these initiatives further, we found that most enterprises sought to transform on two dimensions: (1) to better understand and deliver what their end customers want and (2) to operate in an increasingly coordinated network of enterprises, devices, and customers to create value for all participants. These two dimensions became the axes of the two-by-two framework (our DBM framework).

Most enterprises today don't operate in an ecosystem (as Amazon does) but instead control or participate in a more linear value chain (in which Walmart has traditionally operated). The combination of moving from value chains toward ecosystems and increasing customer knowledge provides leaders with the four distinct business models that we'll explore in detail now.

Each model in the DBM framework shown in figure I-1 has very different characteristics. The horizontal axis signifies the business *design*, moving rightward from a value chain to an ecosystem. The vertical axis is the enterprise's *depth of knowledge* of its end customer.

An important caveat: although enterprises that are both closer to their end customer and earn most of their revenues from ecosystems have, up to now, outperformed their industry-average profitability (by more than 25 percent), an ecosystem driver as a business model is hard to get right. The challenges of becoming a successful ecosystem driver include the need for the enterprise to develop a coordinated set of capabilities and practices—everything that companies in the supplier, omnichannel, and modular-producer models do, and more. Ecosystem drivers must develop a platform that others want to plug into; they also must have great data and sustain a stream of innovation. And because this model has numerous moving parts put together, the enterprise will need robust digital governance that continually enhances, rather than fragments, the platform.[11]

Certainly, therefore, not every enterprise will be able to make the move to ecosystem driver right away. There are good intermediary goals to shoot for—such as opening up the company to more partnerships and learning more about the end customers. All of which is to say that all four quadrants in our DBM framework are viable business models today. Each has its distinct opportunities and challenges; notably, each model currently delivers, on average, different levels of customer satisfaction and financial performance with ecosystem drivers having the best overall performance. But many businesses operate and will continue to operate profitably using a model that isn't an ecosystem driver.

Now let's examine each DBM framework quadrant in turn.

## Suppliers

Firms in this quadrant have, at best, a partial knowledge of their end customers and typically operate in the value chain of another, often more powerful enterprise. Suppliers include enterprises that sell insurance via independent agents (e.g., Chubb Group), electronic goods like TVs via retailers (e.g., Sony), or mutual funds via brokers (e.g., Vanguard). As enterprises continue to digitize, suppliers are likely to lose more power and be pressured to continually reduce prices, perhaps accelerating industry consolidation. P&G—a prime supplier in many other enterprises' value chains—feels this potential loss of power and recent flat growth. To gain more leverage, P&G began a campaign to learn more about, and connect directly to, its more than four billion end customers worldwide, using a variety of branding, social media, direct-to-customer (e.g., Pampers.com) and data-based approaches, effectively moving up in the DBM framework. For example, P&G has built more than fifty visually immersive "business sphere" conference rooms worldwide, the company's executives address a particular business challenge, like increasing Pampers sales in Singapore. Data is collected and displayed in planetarium-like rooms, and the executives do the analysis, debate the evidence, and decide what to do next. A real-time "decision cockpit" can be quickly created, and the impact of the decisions is tracked over the next few weeks and months. P&G is practicing *test and learn*, where it makes evidence-based decisions and then tracks the results on the cockpit—adjusting its course as needed over subsequent weeks. Simultaneously, the company is learning more about its customers in real time.

## *Omnichannels*

Businesses with an omnichannel model provide customers access to their products across multiple channels, including physical and digital channels, delivering greater choice and a seamless experience. BT, Carrefour, Nordstrom, Origin Energy, Walmart, Canadian Imperial Bank of Commerce (CIBC), Citibank, and many others aspire to be great omnichannel businesses controlling an integrated value chain with a strong claim to "own" the customer relationship. The challenge is to move up the vertical axis of the DBM framework, acting on an increased knowledge of the end customers and their goals and life events, and reducing customer churn. Many enterprises we talked to mentioned big-data analytics, social media, sentiment analysis, mobile apps, and measures of customer experience such as net promoter score (NPS) as avenues for increasing their understanding of the end customer. Some enterprises have moved significantly up the vertical axis by rethinking their relationship with their customers and remaking their organization to reflect the changed relationship.

USAA is a $27 billion revenue bank formed in 1922 to serve the US military. Headquartered in San Antonio, Texas, it has never had branches, and with 11.9 million members and a complex set of financial products and services, the company engages its customers increasingly by digital channels. USAA believes that its members' satisfaction is paramount to success, and in an effort to provide superior customer experience, it reconceived its offerings from products like insurance, credit cards, and car loans to meeting the life events of its customers. When connecting to USAA via mobile, web, or phone, you can indicate whether you are experiencing a life event such as buying a car, moving, getting married, or having a child. Each of these life events triggers an integrated package of products designed to meet all the financial needs of that event.

For example, the services the bank could offer customers buying a car include the car purchase itself, a car loan, extended vehicle protection, car insurance, a month-by-month maintenance guide, and the sale of the person's current car.[12] The results of rethinking the business by life events combined with the bank's other customer initiatives are impressive: USAA earned a banking NPS score of 73 (out of 100), compared with an industry average of 35, in 2016.[13] To achieve this groundbreaking customer experience and NPS score, USAA not only relied on a single customer information file and shared infrastructure, data, and application services, but also performed significant organizational surgery. In 2010, USAA integrated its channel and call-center management from four separate lines of business into one organization, Member Experience. This group was trained and focused around life events. Many other banks tout life events in their marketing but have yet to reorganize themselves to achieve USAA's level of customer satisfaction.

## Modular Producers

Businesses that provide plug-and-play products or services that can adapt to any number of ecosystems are modular producers. To survive, they have to be one of the best producers of their core activity (like payments). To thrive, they must constantly innovate their products and services, ensuring that these offerings are among the best options available and at the right price. Modular producers typically operate in a hypercompetitive market, as it's usually easy for customers or a robot to search for an alternative and switch—and the whole point of being a modular producer is being plug-and-play.

PayPal, with 2016 revenues of $10.8 billion, processed a massive $354 billion in transactions. With a five-year compounded annual growth rate of 15.9 percent and a net margin of 12.9 percent, PayPal is a strong and fast-growing business that eBay spun off in 2015. Like any good modular producer, PayPal can operate in virtually any ecosystem, being hardware agnostic, mobile enabled, and platform-based. Equally important, modular producers like PayPal can operate in many countries and can adapt to many legal and compliance environments. For example in 2016, almost half of PayPal's revenues came from outside the United States in over two hundred markets and twenty-five currencies, including Australia, Bermuda, France, Indonesia, Kenya, Peru, Qatar, the United Kingdom, and Ukraine.

Payment management is a hot and highly competitive market-place right now, with many new offerings like Apple Pay and Square as well as many banks offering payments services like PayLah from DBS in Singapore. Although there may be many modular producers, typically only the top three or four make significant profits in each market while the others struggle—as it's ultimately a commodity business. Also, most modular producers—unlike ecosystem drivers—see only part of the customer data, as they are usually limited to processing a single transaction at a time. For example, if you purchase a Vanguard fund through the Fidelity.com's portfolio analysis tool, Vanguard won't see your entire portfolio position but will see only the single purchase transaction for its fund.

## Ecosystem Drivers

Enterprises with this DBM establish a digital ecosystem (a coordinated network of enterprises, devices, and customers to create value for all participants) by fostering relationships with other providers who offer complementary (and sometimes competing) services to their own to more completely meet the needs of customers. Because this model has the best performance on net margin, revenue growth, customer experience, and innovation, becoming an ecosystem driver is the goal for many enterprises.

Ecosystem drivers like Aetna, Amazon, Apple, Fidelity, Microsoft, and WeChat provide a platform for the participants to do business—a more or less open platform, depending on the enterprise. For example, Apple's ecosystem is more closed—like a walled garden—than Google's more open ecosystem. In financial services, Fidelity highlights its own mutual funds but also offers funds from hundreds of competitors and complementors like Vanguard, USAA, and BlackRock. Ecosystem drivers use their brand strength to attract participants, ensure a great customer experience, and offer one-stop shopping. Like omnichannel businesses, they also aspire to "own" the customer relationship by increasing their knowledge of their end customers. But more importantly, ecosystem drivers want to become *the* destination for a subset of their customers. So when customers think of health care and wellness, they think of Aetna; when they think of shopping (and more areas every day), they think of Amazon; and when they think of wealth management, they think of Fidelity.

To appreciate the intensity of the battle to become the dominant ecosystem driver in one very digital domain, just look at the news. Enterprises like Bloomberg, Apple News, Facebook, the Guardian, New York Times, Australian Financial Review, the Straits Times, and the BBC are fighting to establish themselves as the first place that people go for news globally—not just in their home markets. And in many markets, Facebook—not a news company—is gaining traction as a news provider since it has so many regular users. And this desire to be *the* destination applies equally to B2B customers. Schneider Electric wants to be the first place its customers think of for energy management and automation needs. LexisNexis aims to be the first destination that lawyers consider for their information and search requirements.

An ecosystem driver offers a full range of services to a subset of its customers from both its own capabilities and those of its partners. Ecosystem drivers extract rents from the participants in their ecosystem—both customers and service providers—and rely on brand strength, great data, and customer ratings to build reputation and usage. For example, Aetna, a $60 billion managed health-care enterprise serving both individuals and employers, has a vision to become a health-care destination; this vision helped propel the company's 12 percent annual growth over the five years up to 2015. Besides being part of many public-health exchanges, Aetna would like to become the place that a subset of customers heads to for more and more of their health and wellness needs. To reach this goal, Aetna would need to move its business from primarily B2B (managing enterprises' health-care plans) to B2B2C (managing enterprises' health-care plans and interacting with the end customer directly) and to B2C (direct health-care solutions to end customers) while learning more about its customers' health and wellness needs. Aetna is increasingly focusing on a multiproduct and multiservice customer experience that integrates its own products with third parties, like health and nutrition coaches, and other related services, such as credit cards.

## Moving Your Business Up and to the Right

Once you've determined where your company stands in the DBM framework, the next step is to decide which quadrant you can reasonably aim toward to deal with the threat of digital disruption and create new opportunities for the enterprise. We recommend that at some point you experiment with becoming an ecosystem driver for least some of your best customers. The capabilities you develop as you try this will serve your enterprise well in the other digital models. (For one company's story, see the sidebar "Schneider Electric Rethinks Its Business Model.")

To grasp the potential of digitization, enterprises today must move up and right on the DBM framework. They need to learn more about their end customers *and* change their business design to emphasize more partnering and more porous boundaries toward becoming ecosystems drivers. Yet most businesses find themselves on the left side of the framework. Among the larger companies we studied (those with more than $1 billion in annual revenues), 46 percent were suppliers, 24 percent were omnichannel, 18 percent were modular producers, and 12 percent were ecosystem drivers.

Interestingly, smaller enterprises (revenues less than $1 billion) are already further up and to the right on the DBM framework than larger enterprises are, with 31 percent in the ecosystem-driver model and 36 percent in the omnichannel model (18 percent were suppliers and 15 percent were modular producers). Why are smaller businesses becoming such effective digital disrupters? Digitization is the vehicle for enterprises to create a strong connection with their end customers (moving up), and with other companies and suppliers that they partner with (moving right), to meet more of the customer's needs. This customer connection can be through websites, social media, mobile apps, or, for partners, API-links to the ecosystem driver's internal enterprise systems, like the claims systems in an insurance company. Data analytics and testing and learning what works and what doesn't work through online experimentation helps refine the customer engagement. Typically becoming more of an ecosystem model requires taking what makes you great as an enterprise—your own crown jewels—and making them available through digital

## Schneider Electric Rethinks Its Business Model

Schneider Electric has evolved to lead the digital transformation of energy management and automation, with the mission of ensuring that "'Life Is On' for everyone, everywhere, and at every moment."[a] In 2009, Schneider Electric shifted its strategic focus from "manufacturer and distributor of electrical and automation products" (its "supplier model") to "provider of intelligent energy management and automation solutions" (an "ecosystem driver"). From a customer perspective, Schneider Electric's offerings have evolved from a collection of complex, often stand-alone electrical and mechanical products to a portfolio of end-to-end solutions of connected, intelligent devices; edge control; and apps, analytics, and services. Its IoT-enabled energy management and automation solutions are able to constantly monitor the environment and systems, proactively detect faults or changes needed, enable operators to take action in real time, and empower business decision makers with data-based insights. Those solutions are able in addition to leverage a cloud platform in order to access new types of digital services from optimization to benchmark to preventative assets maintenance.

Even more important from a future-success perspective, customers are getting end-to-end solutions and Schneider Electric is taking better advantage of its expertise and assets located in different parts of the enterprise. Chairman & CEO Jean-Pascal Tricoire explains: "Over the past ten years, Schneider Electric's value proposition has shifted from bringing safe energy to every office, every home, every machine, every infrastructure to a value proposition that is much more comprehensive."

Schneider Electric developed solutions that combined energy technology with information technology. The company stepped up its move to IoT solutions in 2009, with the introduction of its first-generation "EcoStruxure" intelligent energy management solutions. In 2010, solutions growth accelerated to 12 percent, and, in 2012, 39 percent of Schneider Electric's revenues came from solutions instead of products.[b] The results of the business model transformation have been impressive, with 2016 revenue of 24.7 billion euros—44 percent from its IoT-enabled solutions.[c]

a. The information on the history and transformation of Schneider Electric comes from our interviews and conversations with senior Schneider Electric executives, particularly CIO Hervé Coureil and CEO Jean-Pascal Tricoire; our presentation at a digital strategy retreat in Hong Kong, 2011; N. Fonstad and J. Ross, "Building Business Agility: Cloud-Based Services and Digitized Platform Maturity," *Massachusetts Institute of Technology, Sloan School of Management, Center for Information Systems Research (MIT CISR) Briefing* 15, no. 2 (February 2015); A. Karunakaran, J. Mooney, and J. W. Ross, "Accelerating Global Digital Platform Deployment Using the Cloud: A Case Study of Schneider Electric's 'Bridge Front Office' Program," working paper 399 MIT CISR, Cambridge, MA, January 2015); S. Scantlebury "Redesigning Schneider Electric's Operating Model," case vignette, MIT CISR, Cambridge, MA, 2015; and Schneider Electric, "Mobile and Tablet Applications," *Life Is On* (Schneider Electric blog), accessed October 22, 2017, www.schneider-electric.co.uk/en/work/support/apps.

b. Schneider Electric 2010 Annual Report; Schneider Electric 2012 Annual Report.

c. Schneider Electric 2016 Annual Report.

services to other enterprises. Smaller, newer companies are often designed that way from the beginning.

Many smaller companies remain nimble by avoiding the temptation to create entire solutions themselves. Instead, they offer solutions created from services developed by other companies (e.g., an offering that relies on a mapping service from Google and a payment service from PayPal, coupled with one of their own services). And these smaller companies have fewer legacy systems and are more willing to take a risk with their business model. They also are more able to collect, analyze, and act on the data required to really know their end customers. Larger enterprises have more of this data, but often don't exploit it as successfully. One reason smaller enterprises have been more agile, particularly around data, is that many were born digital and have designed their systems, processes, and, most importantly, their evidence-based cultures to be more connected both to their end customers and to their partners.

The smaller enterprises' instincts are well founded. Such enterprises—which derive more revenues from ecosystems than from other business models and have invested in better customer knowledge (i.e., further up and to the right on the DBM framework)—enjoy statistically significantly higher margins than do their competitors.[14] Part of the reason for their better margins is that smaller enterprises are measurably more responsive to their customers' needs than are larger firms, and they collaborate with other enterprises to meet those needs.

Now let's look closer at the hows and whys of each business model's performance outcome. Figure I-2 in the introduction shows the average results for net margin and growth and two important factors for future performance—customer experience and time to market—for each business model.[15] In all four metrics, ecosystem drivers

are the highest performers, followed by omnichannels or modular producers. And last on all these metrics are suppliers. Suppliers still make money but have less margin and lower growth than do ecosystem drivers operating in the same industry. Suppliers should buy options—investments now that create future opportunities—to move up and to the right even if those options won't increase profitability and growth immediately. There are benefits to learning more about customers and learning more about partnering with another enterprise's platform. That's why Procter & Gamble is creating more of an omnichannel business by engaging directly with end customers—through websites like Pampers.com, social media, sentiment analysis, and communities organized around specific topics or concerns (for example, P&G shares information about its health brands through its "Health Community" and encourages community participation through activities like photo contests). Many omnichannel businesses are also buying options to move right on the DBM framework (from the value chain toward an ecosystem) to create ecosystem-driver businesses for a subset of their customers—say for an insurance company to become the go-to destination for homeownership for a group of its customers.

In chapter 1, we described the three digital-exploiting approaches that enterprises can use to compete: a new offering, a new business model, or new capabilities that facilitate crossing industry boundaries. Any one of these approaches for an established enterprise creates an opportunity to move out of the supplier business model toward the more lucrative business models: ecosystem drivers, omnichannels, and modular producers in an industry. However, disruptors, that is, new entrants into an industry (either startups or companies crossing industry boundaries), are also more likely to aim for those same business models. This increased competition will make it even more difficult for suppliers (and existing omnichannel enterprises) to move up and to the right. While industry shakeouts are not yet widespread (though two clear examples in the United States are media and now retail), we are confident that there will be competitive battles in all customer domains, like health care, financial management and entertainment.

As enterprises struggle to grow their competitive advantage only 12 percent of large enterprises are currently ecosystem drivers (with about half of large enterprises operating primarily as suppliers). As large enterprises try to become ecosystem drivers, two interesting trends are emerging. First, we expect that enterprises' attempts to become ecosystem drivers will lead to a consolidation in several industries. For example, how many successful ecosystem drivers can there be in each customer domain? Each customer is likely to choose one go-to ecosystem driver for shopping, for example, and will choose one ecosystem driver for each additional area of life such as financial management, entertainment, and health care. Sure, we as customers may shop around, but just as Amazon is the default stop for many shoppers, this trend toward consolidation is continuing in other domains. And not just for B2C, but also for B2B firms. For instance, we've already seen significant consolidation of foreign-exchange providers. The number of traders employed in Europe dropped 30 percent from 2013 to 2016, partly because of tighter regulation.[16] As big banks reduce their interactions with enterprises making risky trades, there are fewer players in the market.

The second trend is emerging with modular producers. A modular producer like PayPal offers plug-and-play products or services that can adapt to any number of ecosystems. To survive, the company will have to be one of the best producers in a narrow domain, such as payments. We expect to see the top three or four players dominate in each niche, with the many other players picking up the scraps. These top few players will be highly profitable, but the average profitability for modular producers will diminish over time.

There are also different distributions of the four models across industries. Retail and IT services have the highest percentage of ecosystems, while manufacturing and service industries are still early in their move up and to the right on the DBM framework. It will be easier to create new ecosystem drivers in manufacturing and services than in, say, retail, given that manufacturing is a less crowded space.

The analysis of the threat to your enterprise described in chapter 1 and the discussion of business-model options in this chapter should trigger important decisions for senior management: How urgently and aggressively should your enterprise pursue new business options for its future success? And where is your enterprise now, and where does it want to be?

One part of the self-assessment in chapter 1 addresses the question of urgency: What percentage of your revenues is under threat from digitization over the next five years? We have found that senior teams typically disagree on the threat level at first. The wide variations among individual estimates are usually debated until the team collectively agrees on the level of threat—often by sorting out differing terminology.

If the team's final answer to the threat level posed by digital is more than 30 percent, you need to be buying options now for the future by experimenting with new offerings. If your answer is 50 percent or higher, you should make significant changes to your business model and organizational structure to commit the enterprise to a new way of operating.

## *Creating Options for the Future*

Once a management team has a bead on where it stands in the DBM framework today, the next question is which options it wants to consider for the future to move as much as possible toward becoming an ecosystem driver. In our fifty-plus workshops for C-level executive teams, we've noted that the higher the perceived threat from digital disruption, the more radical the changes that will be needed for the enterprise—and the harder it is for the senior team to make these decisions themselves. The executives often stumble here because it's their own organizations, direct reports, and global teams that will be most affected, not to mention their own power bases, compensation, and status.

In a recent executive team workshop we ran for a media enterprise, the team members identified the current position for the dominant model as just above the border between supplier and omnichannel. This enterprise produces leading paper and digital newspapers in several markets, along with active news websites and specialty online destinations for specific interests like cars, houses, and travel. The team agreed that over the next five years, approximately 70 percent of its revenues would be under threat from digital disruption. And disruption has already taken a toll on all traditional media enterprises' revenues. Print runs for paper newspapers are declining, and although online subscriptions are growing, the net effect on revenue is negative. Why? As competition for attention and news dissemination grows, so does competition for the related advertising from both specialty enterprises and giants like Apple News and Facebook.

For example, Apple News allows readers to customize their news outlets and then receive a steady stream of the top stories from all those outlets at no direct cost. Even more subtly, if you click a Facebook "like" from a particular news organization, then you start receiving its news bulletins in your Facebook feed. The senior team in the media enterprise we worked with saw the threat clearly. "We can't afford to not be involved with Apple News and Facebook," one executive concluded, "but we need to make sure we make money overall, and how to do that is not [expletive deleted] clear to me." For this media enterprise, quantifying the threat level and identifying where the business currently lies on the DBM framework helped the team narrow down its options. In this case, it had a couple of fast-growing digital destination sites (e.g., a popular auto site) that could be developed further into an ecosystem driver by partnering with car sellers, car servicing, and financing organizations. Alternatively or in addition, the enterprise could offer elements of the car site as a modular producer to a broader ecosystem driver, like a bank.

A good solution we've seen for many enterprises is first to make investments that move them up the vertical axis (improving end-customer knowledge) of the DBM framework. They do this by enhancing the collection, consolidation, and generation of insights about their customers—resulting in better customer experience and more targeted and successful offers. They then venture to the right, moving from a series of interactions where they provide services directly to the customer to a web of relationships that provide a broader set of services using partners.

USAA moved up the vertical axis with its life-event strategy, and now the company is moving right. With Auto Circle (the service developed around the life event of purchasing a car), USAA helps its customers find their perfect car, links them to car dealers with the desired cars in stock, negotiates the price, provides financing, and sometimes facilitates delivery. The average saving for a USAA member is $3,385 off the recommended retail price. We can imagine

USSA extending the use of third parties to broaden the services provided for many of their customers' life events, like buying a house.

BBVA, the Spanish-based global bank, is hoping to learn more about its customers by investing heavily in new-style consultative branches, ATMs, and a new digital banking model, all of which should also improve the customer experience while keeping costs low via automation. At the same time, BBVA expects to move to the right on the DBM framework (toward ecosystems) to explore collaboration with other players. BBVA can choose whether to brand its core banking services and become an ecosystem driver by incorporating additional third-party services on its platform.

In chapter 5, we will return to the DBM framework and describe the four capabilities required for your enterprise to move up and four additional capabilities required to move to the right.

## Aetna: Becoming an Ecosystem Driver

Given that ecosystem drivers are the most successful model we've seen for companies today, let's examine one company's journey to become an ecosystem driver and the destination for its end customers.

Several years ago, Aetna recognized that the current health-care ecosystem was primed for disruption: enterprises that insured their employees faced rising costs, customers' out-of-pocket expenses were increasing, and providers were being compensated for volume rather than rewarded for value. Worse still, Aetna pointed out that with a customer-experience rating below that of hotels, airlines, and cable TV providers, health insurers were ill-prepared for the direct-to-customer environment.

The rise of health-care exchanges in the United States—a result of the Affordable Care Act of 2010 (legislation currently being changed)—gave people, many who had not previously had access to affordable health insurance, fundamentally new and different ways to enroll in health-care plans. Aetna began participating in some of the exchanges. The realization that health care is being disrupted and the creation of alternative ways of accessing health insurance was the impetus for Aetna to adopt a new vision: *to build a healthier world*. These transformative digital visions really grab customers and say, "We are offering you something great and different." As part of that vision, Aetna seeks to be the most attractive destination to meet the needs of customers and to provide the integrated services that ensure a great customer experience.

Over fifteen years, Aetna's digital strategy moved the enterprise from a supplier of health insurance (in 2000) to an omnichannel business enabling customers to interact with it easily on multiple channels (2010), to an ecosystem driver (2015). Being a successful ecosystem driver required building digital capabilities to broker connections between the enterprise, its customers, and its partners. We will review the key capabilities Aetna built to become an ecosystem driver in chapter 5.

To be an effective ecosystem driver, Aetna needed to become an attractive destination for health and wellness needs—with a much broader system of relationships, partnerships, and services—and not just provide health insurance. To make the transformation, Aetna had to develop a clear vision—"to build a healthier world"—that was more expansive than selling insurance. The vision gave Aetna more opportunities to engage with its end customers, integrating a series of acquisitions and partnerships and opening up Aetna's business capabilities so that others could connect. However, Aetna's future as an ecosystem driver will take a new twist given its pending acquisition by CVS.

We have examined in this chapter four business models available in today's increasingly digitized world. And we have pointed out that digitization will make businesses more open and networked and, with increasing competition and consolidation, will move enterprises up and to the right on the DBM framework, making them more ecosystem-driven.

Where does your enterprise now reside on the DBM framework? Where do you want to move? We recommend that every enterprise create opportunities for the future by experimenting with becoming an ecosystem driver for least some of its best customers. Without having a successful ecosystem-driver business, the only viable option in a digital world is to become a modular producer—a very competitive business model with more easily replaced products and services. Will you become an Amazon or a seller on Amazon? As one of our workshop participants so eloquently put it, "It's all about who's going to become the head of the snake."

Next, we explore ways that you can identify and capitalize on your enterprise's sources of competitive advantage. With so many new competitors in the digital economy, understanding and building on exactly what makes your company great will put you ahead of your competitors.

**CHAPTER 3**

# What Is Your Digital Competitive Advantage?

Way back in 2011, 72 percent of mobile-app customers said that if the capability became available, they would replace some of the traditional channels they used with mobile apps.[1] Today, nearly 60 percent of spending on digital media (desktop, mobile web, and mobile apps) is spent in mobile apps.[2] With apps set to become the primary channel for customer engagement in most industries, many companies are adopting mobile-first or mobile-only strategies and disrupting competitors all around them. For instance, a recent study of one hundred of Europe's largest retailers reports that 90 percent have a mobile-first mentality or are moving toward that.[3]

Not only does digitization today empower customers to interact with companies whenever and wherever they choose, but it also enhances consumer knowledge and choice as never before. Digitization enables customers to search and evaluate digital descriptions of products through images, third-party product ratings, and objective facts like specifications and features. When shopping for services, too, consumers are at the controls with a variety of options: you can plan travel using a search engine like Bing, a website like TripAdvisor, or an intermediary like Expedia, all of which often incorporate customers' shared experience via ratings and social media—before deciding on your purchase.

These many changes have converged to raise the stakes for how well your enterprise engages customers and deals with digital disruption. And getting better at digitally engaging your customers pays off. Enterprises in the top third of our measure of digital customer experience had 8.5 percent higher net profit margins and 7.8 percent higher revenue growth than their competitors.[4]

To compete in today's intricately networked, consumer-driven environment, leaders need to understand where their enterprise's competitive advantage lies. That is the third question we asked in the introduction to this book. By answering the first two questions from the previous chapters—determining the enterprise's digital threat level and selecting your most effective future business model—you laid the groundwork for identifying your competitive advantage. That knowledge will help you advance your business model steadily up and to the right on our DBM framework for the new digital enterprise.

Our research shows that competitive advantage comes from one (or more) of three sources:

- Content: products and information

- Customer experience: the quality of the interaction between customers and your content, which is influenced by your content's ease of use and the way it is presented to the customer, often bundled synergistically (i.e., as a multiproduct offering) and across multiple channels

- **Platforms:** the way your content is delivered to customers through a set of internal digitized processes, data, and infrastructure, as well as external services (figure 3-1)

Maintaining a practice of refreshing and enriching *content* drives new sources of revenue. Creating a superior *customer experience* helps drive cross-selling and increased revenue per customer. And by developing digitized *platforms* and reusing them (sharing across the enterprise rather than reinventing for each area), an enterprise achieves economies of scale with better margins.[5]

**FIGURE 3-1**

## What is your competitive advantage?

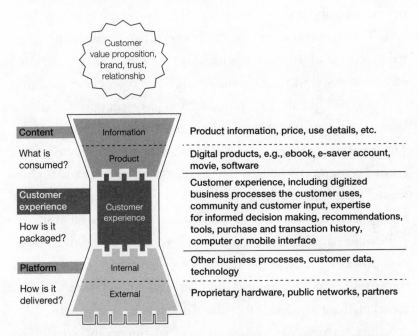

*Source:* Adapted from P. Weill and M. Vitale, *Place to Space: Migrating to eBusiness Models* (Boston: Harvard Business School Press, 2001); and J. Rayport and J. Sviokla, "Managing in the Marketspace," *Harvard Business Review*, November–December 1994; and P. Weill and S. L. Woerner, "Optimizing Your Digital Business Model," *Sloan Management Review*, spring 2013. © 2017 MIT Sloan Center for Information Systems Research. Used with permission.

At the end of this chapter, you'll find a self-assessment to assess how good your content, customer experience, and platforms are and which of these sources of competitive advantage will be the primary driver of your transformation. Whatever your competitive advantage turns out to be, make no mistake, you need to identify and expand on it. Otherwise, your customers, particularly younger people, will move to industry competitors or do more business with enterprises like Amazon—or any enterprise that provides superior customer experiences while operating in adjacent industries and offering services similar to yours.

Consider how Amazon makes the most of all three sources of competitive advantage. Amazon's content—what is consumed—includes digital products like movies and software, as well as information about the physical and digital products it sells or brokers. The customer experience embodies what it's like to be a digital customer of your enterprise. Amazon's customer experience includes the website and the digitized business processes touching the customer, like the shopping cart and payment options, as well as messaging, such as delivery alerts and email acknowledgments. The experience also includes Amazon's well-developed customer-created content: customer product ratings and reviews and sophisticated tools like search, a detailed history of purchases, Amazon Pantry service, recent searches, and tailored recommendations.

Finally, Amazon's platform—a coherent set of digitized business processes, data, and infrastructures—delivers the content to the customer and has internal and external components.[6] The internal platforms include customer data and all the non-customer-touching business processes, such as customer analytics, HR, finance, and merchandising. External platforms include the phones, tablets, or computers that customers use to research and purchase the products, along with telecommunications networks and Amazon's partnership with delivery enterprises like UPS, which generates text messages concerning delivery. All these external platforms neatly integrate with Amazon's internal platforms.

As described earlier, Amazon is a leading ecosystem driver in the DBM framework. An effective ecosystem driver must have world-class capabilities in all three competitive capabilities. Companies that operate in one (or more) of the other three models in the framework—supplier, omnichannel, and modular producer—require a different combination of excellence in the areas of content, customer experience, or platforms. Later in this chapter, we will further explore those advantages for each of the models in the framework.

Like Amazon, your enterprise eventually will need to be superior in all three sources of competitive advantage to compete in the digital economy of the future. But building capabilities in content, customer experience, and platforms simultaneously is a Herculean task. For now, especially if you are a born-physical enterprise making the digital transition, focus on just one or two areas as you begin creating your next-generation enterprise, keeping in mind the following:

- If your goal is driving new digital revenue, then start with strengthening your digital content.

- If your goal is cross-selling and driving more revenue per customer, focus on improving your digital customer experience.

- If your goal is efficiency and flexibility, then focus on building and exploiting your shared digital platforms.

(For more on coordinating your strategic goals with the sources of competitive advantage, see the sidebar "Where Should You Begin Building Your Capabilities?")

## Where Should You Begin Building Your Capabilities?

The place to start depends on your strategic goals for your next-generation enterprise. To attract new revenue, you need a steady stream of new, attractive content—new products, new features, new information. For example, banks, telcos, and media companies are constantly presenting new offerings (e.g., credit-card features, phone plans, and songs) to drive customer buzz and to increase both digital and physical channel revenues. But the customer experience is what drives a higher share of revenues from the digital channel and more revenue per customer. Like the offerings at Amazon and others, a rich customer experience, including easy-to-use interfaces, the ability to self-serve, and input from fellow customers, makes customers more loyal to the online channel and spend more money in it. But platforms are what drive lower costs. If lower costs and best margins are your primary driver, then start with platforms.

If you are focused on digital, and your enterprise's goal is being an industry leader in generating profits from digital products and services, then you need to be superior at all three capabilities, not just one of them. For strong digital profits, the combination of all three makes a difference: content (to attract buzz and grow revenues), customer experience (to please customers and cross-sell), and platforms (to flexibly achieve scale economies).

This chapter will show you how to further identify and capitalize on your best sources of competitive advantage, drawing on results from a Massachusetts Institute of Technology Center for Information Systems Research at the Sloan School of Management (MIT CISR) effective-practices survey of top-performing companies as well as case studies from digital leaders like Amazon, BBVA, CBA, Fidelity, LexisNexis, Netflix, Schneider Electric, TripAdvisor, and DBS.

We begin with a discussion of the shift from *place* to *space* that has been driven by digitization and how enterprises' competitive advantages have been affected by the shift. Next we examine content, customer experience, and platforms, followed by a description of which competitive advantages are most useful for each business model in our framework. Then we offer a case study of a company that uses all three advantages to boost competitiveness: LexisNexis. A self-assessment at the chapter's end will help you identify the most important source or sources of competitive advantage for your next-generation enterprise.

## Competitive Advantage and the Shift from Place to Space

Before the internet, businesses operated primarily in a physical world of *place*: tangible, product based, and customer-transaction oriented. To delight customers, businesses relied on places—such as bank branches, department stores, university classrooms, and medical clinics—and people, in the form of sales teams, insurance agents, store clerks, teachers, and doctors.

Today, all industries—moving at different rates—are shifting toward a world of digital *space*. Their offerings are more intangible, more service based, and more customer-experience oriented, with business conducted largely through computers, mobile devices, and apps.[7]

Your enterprise needs to examine how it will move from place to space and engage customers digitally. Delighting a customer in your space and enhancing digital engagement requires re-thinking three main areas inside the enterprise. *Internal account-ability* (who "owns" the customers) often changes from product owners—like the credit-card group in a bank—to the unit that manages the multiproduct customer experience. *Business processes* need rethinking to allow automated self-service and seamless ac-cess across channels. And *customer data* must become accessible enterprise-wide. The stakes are high; so you don't want to get these areas wrong.

Just look at Netflix in 2011, an enterprise that dominated the DVD mail rental business and had strong claims on the video streaming business. Through a business-model misstep—coupling a large price hike with the separation of the physical busi-ness model (mail) from the digital business model (streaming)—the Netflix team annoyed many of its customers. The result was a 79 percent drop in share price from July 2011 to November 2011, despite 52 percent revenue growth. The stock market lost confi-dence in Netflix's ability to manage the enterprise. Reed Hast-ings, Netflix CEO, realized that the company tried to do too much too fast.[8] He apologized, via a letter to subscribers, a blog post on the company website, and a YouTube video, explaining in detail what Netflix was trying to accomplish.[9] Netflix has since rebounded and is arguably leading the world in online streaming entertainment, having made a major expansion globally in 2015 and a significant investment in great content—for example, exclu-sive licensing from Disney and investments in original content.

By first quarter 2017, it had reached almost one hundred million subscribers.[10] And Netflix's stock price has since skyrocketed to more than ten times the 2011 low, showing how fast a successful digital business can rise, fall, and then rise again.

The *Wall Street Journal* (WSJ) offers another example. In the former world of place, WSJ produced its own content (stories, photos, etc.), packaged it into a printed newspaper (with a distinctive look, feel, and editorial style), and delivered it via a custom-built infrastructure (printing presses, trucks, and delivery people). Customer value was produced via a tight integration of these components.

In the new world of space, the components of content, packaging, and infrastructure have morphed and split. Content has mushroomed and is no longer strictly proprietary: WSJ obtains branded content from other sources (like Reuters) and provides its content to partners to deliver to their customers. The packaging has been transformed into a consistent digital customer experience, including search, save, and other useful features available on many different devices. Infrastructure has been developed into a powerful combination of internal and external digital platforms—some controlled by WSJ and some not (e.g., you can access WSJ on your phone, PC, and TV from anywhere). Customer value is now produced via a modular combination of these components, often creating different value propositions for each customer.

As we have seen in the move from print news to digital, once the tipping point is reached, the movement to space speeds up and is hard to resist. Other industries will follow at different paces, driven, in part, by issues like regulation, product complexity, and how amenable the products are to digitization. Even in industries like health care, which traditionally relies on the physical

## Competitive Advantage by Industry

How effectively you exploit the three competitive levers depends partly on your enterprise's industry. To better understand best practices by industry, we surveyed companies to assess the effectiveness of their content, customer experience, and platform and looked for impacts on enterprise performance and industry differences.

The industry with the strongest effectiveness scores overall was IT software and services. Energy, mining, and health care were among the poorest. Notably, in each industry, the top financial performers—on a combination of net margin and growth—also had better scores on all three competitive levers. For example, in the financial services industry, the top third of financial performers had 29 percent, 35 percent, and 26 percent better content, customer experience, and platform scores, respectively, than did the bottom third performers. These results provide good evidence that enterprises with stronger digital competitive advantage also have stronger financial performance.

Moreover, we are seeing companies in the same industries move in cohorts through major shifts in digital transformation. For example, in banking ten or more years ago, the focus was on content. Back then, banking was a product play where banks competed on product innovation and features, providing more and different products to customers. Big investments were made to create the best mortgage, credit card, or car loan. Today and for the last decade or so, product innovation and features have become less of a source of advantage, since most banks have lots of products and complex offerings. Instead, many banks around the world have focused on building flexible platforms such as core banking systems that allow product changes and innovative product offerings (like family plans) to be made more easily and at lower costs, allowing banks to target and react to customers more effectively. This focus on platforms helped banks reduce their cost-to-income ratios (the ratio of operating expenses to operating income—a common measure of banking efficiency) from as high as 75 percent to industry-leading levels of around 35 percent.[a]

Banking today has also shifted toward improving customer experience. Customers don't just want a great mortgage; they want a great multiproduct experience—integrated and provided through their mobile device, computer, personal banker, or bank branch—which should create a better, stronger relationship between customers and their banks. This kind of change creates the need for major surgery in organizations, often breaking the relationship between the individual product providers (e.g., credit cards or mortgage) and the customer and adding a multichannel customer-experience group between the product owner and the customer.

a. "Tightened belts loosen due to income crisis," *thebanker.com*, June 7, 2010, http://www.thebanker.com/Banker-Data/Banker-Rankings/Tightened-belts-loosen-due-to-income-crisis. Graphic of best cost-to-income ratios of top 50 banks worldwide, www.thebanker.com/var/ezflow_site/storage/images/media/images/best-cost-to-income-ratios-of-top-50-banks-worldwide/6106060-1-eng-GB/Best-Cost-to-income-ratios-of-Top-50-banks-worldwide.jpg.

interaction between provider and patient, we are seeing more on-line services: physicians can now provide advice over secure email and monitor patients remotely; Aetna offered iTriage, a smart-phone app that gave users access to extensive health care, diag-nosis, and medical information; and insurance companies enable online claims with more and more self-service. The move from place to space and the need for a digital competitive advantage is not just a phenomenon limited to the customer market. B2B en-terprises will be just as affected, though perhaps at a slower pace. (For more discussion on how well different kinds of industries use various competitive advantages, see the sidebar "Competitive Advantage by Industry.")

## Competing on Content

To achieve new revenue growth in a DBM, companies need qual-ity content that addresses customer needs and is refreshed often. Customers return and engage when there is interesting and new content on a site, increasing revenues for the enterprise. Those revenues give the company opportunities to develop better ways of providing the content (the platform) and more varied ways of involving the customer in the consumption (the customer experi-ence). Companies that skimp on their content or have stale con-tent that lacks buzz have lower growth. As we'll describe later, one model in our framework—supplier—is particularly able to use content to maximum competitive advantage. For now, let's consider how TripAdvisor has moved toward an ecosystem busi-ness model—a one-stop travel destination—becoming probably the best-known and world's largest travel enterprise, operating in forty-nine markets and twenty-eight languages.[11]

TripAdvisor's content includes more than five hundred million restaurant, hotel, and attraction reviews, photos, rating, rankings, maps, prices, and availability information. With 455 average million unique users per month, TripAdvisor has seriously disrupted the travel industry, particularly travel agents, guidebook publishers, and travel reviewers.[12] What's more, with TripAdvisor's purchase of HouseTrip in 2016, it has begun to broaden its content to compete with Airbnb.[13]

Leveraging the company's stellar content is TripAdvisor's terrific customer experience, including powerful capabilities such as meta-search, online booking, city guides, vacation calculators, travel forums, and search results integrated with maps. TripAdvisor realized that customers used the web portal to plan trips and its mobile app to guide them when they arrived at their destinations. To support both content and customer experience, TripAdvisor has a strong global platform that connects partners to the site and links a customer's online and mobile use, all seamlessly.

Nevertheless, the company's content remains the reason that users come back repeatedly. TripAdvisor CEO Steve Kaufer explains: "It's that content piece that even our extremely well-funded competitors can't magically create. And that just becomes an incredible barrier to entry."[14]

Another positive impact is that TripAdvisor made hotels and restaurants much more accountable to customers. Hotel and restaurant managers often reply to both positive and critical TripAdvisor user reviews within hours of posting. TripAdvisor derives most of its revenues from advertising and fees for bookings. The result is that TripAdvisor has a five-year revenue growth of 18.4 percent—with a 2016 net profit margin of 8.1 percent—compared with an industry average of 15.9 percent on revenues of US$1.5 billion.[15]

## Competing on Customer Experience

To deeply engage customers in a DBM, a company needs to create a superior customer experience. It must continually monitor what customers are doing and what they say they want. It needs to invest in good user interfaces and to create opportunities for collaboration with its customers. Without those elements, a company will fail in its efforts to delight its customers (and customers may be vocal in their irritation) and achieve meaningful cross-selling (an important source of new revenues) and revenue growth per customer.

We'll show later in this chapter how our framework's omnichannel business model uses customer experience to particular competitive advantage. Here, let's consider the omnichannel model of DBS as an example.

DBS, headquartered in Singapore with $7.3 billion in revenues, is among the larger banks in Asia and was identified as the best digital bank globally by Euromoney for 2016.[16] As is the case for many enterprises not born on the web, the creation of a great digital customer experience has been a journey requiring the collaboration of many enterprise units that were previously siloed. In 2009, DBS's reputation for slow response times and otherwise poor customer service provoked a transformation of the bank. DBS redesigned itself, building a core banking platform into which it could integrate the most innovative technologies, creating the ability to react quickly to customers. Placing customers at the center of the banking experience led to an emphasis on customer journeys, optimizing processes and an initiative DBS called RED: "We are Respectful, we making banking Easy, we are Dependable." Enacting these principles made DBS employees feel as if they were creating value rather than cutting costs. And the employees did create value for customers, saving more than one hundred million hours of customer time and reducing queue times by 50 percent.

DBS is now working on making banking "joyful" for customers. The enterprise is becoming more and more customer-centric by focusing on customer journeys (DBS has currently identified 250 such journeys). A customer journey is all the times a customer interacts with your company while completing a particular transaction. Sometimes the journey is mapped for a single interaction, other times the journey is for the entire customer engagement (for example, from onboarding to loan payoff). A journey includes customer actions, motivations, and obstacles. Identifying and diagraming customer journeys is a strong tool for improving the customer experience.[17]

DBS has very good products and platforms, but what drives it as an enterprise is its dedication to providing the best customer experience and every employee's passion to serve customers. That is why the company transformed itself to focus on delivering a great customer experience—and used the saved customer-hours as a unifying metric. The next step for DBS was to expand its brand into a new market, India. There it launched a mobile-only bank called Digibank, which might just paint a picture of the future model of banking everywhere: customers can go to a partner café chain to register, using their government-issued ID card, and then immediately receive an outstanding banking experience on their mobile device. In a year DBS's Digibank has gained more than a million customers in India.[18] (For another example of competing on customer experience, see the sidebar "Schneider Electric's Competitive Advantage.")

## Schneider Electric's Competitive Advantage

As Schneider Electric grew rapidly throughout the early 2000s, many different go-to-market models were developed, and some of its businesses used more than one. As a result, the expertise needed to solve specific, case-by-case client challenges was not always easily accessible to the sales and deliveries teams. Schneider Electric's goal, therefore, was to capitalize on its strengths in energy management—strengths that had been created over time and decentralized to enable local value creation—in order to make its capabilities and expertise available to every customer worldwide. Despite this charge to drive energy management leadership across its markets, a key question for senior executives remained: What was the main source of competitive advantage moving forward?

One of us (PW) remembers vividly speaking at a strategy retreat for the Schneider Electric senior executives in Hong Kong in 2012. There was huge excitement in the room about digital's potential for new value creation at Schneider Electric while still using the core strengths of the enterprise. When asked what the best source of competitive advantage would be in three years, Schneider Electric's executives responded with overwhelming agreement: world-class customer experience. This mutual call to action would require substantial work on the product offerings and digitized platforms, but customer experience was the choice for the company's number one source of competitive advantage in the digital era.

Schneider Electric therefore embarked on a three-year internal company transformation program called "One Schneider." It connected a diverse set of assets, platforms, people, and brand identity after the company's years of acquisitions. The goal was to create a central identity for the enterprise so employees across all levels and departments could act in unison to deliver a great customer experience. To this end, the One Schneider program created a highly collaborative, customer-centric work environment.

One of Schneider Electric's challenges was that through acquisitions it had accumulated more than 150 enterprise resource planning systems and 350 customer relationship management (CRM) systems in different business units. To address this challenge, Schneider Electric established a new global function called Information, Processes and Organization (IPO). This group concluded that Schneider Electric needed a new 360-degree view of the customer and therefore a unified global CRM. Previous experiences in creating in-house shared platforms at Schneider Electric and other large enterprises had often taken five or more years, with mixed results. Schneider needed a faster, more flexible approach, so it opted for a software-as-a-service cloud solution. Two guiding principles were applied: "Go fast, go good enough" and "Deploy only standard functionalities and limit customizations." Schneider Electric IPO implemented the CRM platform in eighteen months at twenty-five thousand field sites in a hundred countries. Connecting all the sales units on the same platform with the same information was important for creating a great customer experience. This platform has been a major enabler of the 20 percent increase in revenues from cross-selling.

## Competing on Platforms

To achieve economies of scale with DBMs, companies need to develop and reuse (sharing across the enterprise rather than reinventing for each area) digitized platforms. Without platforms, the IT units in companies might implement a new solution in response to every business need, creating a spaghetti-like arrangement of systems that meet the current need but are expensive and fragile and don't scale enterprise-wide. Worse still, the customer experience suffers as the customer gets a fragmented, product-based experience rather than a unified, multiproduct experience. Think about your online banking experience today, where you can see all your accounts in one place—and remember what it was like before, when you received individual paper statements for each account.

Later in this chapter, we'll look closely at how one business model in our framework, modular producers, exploits platforms particularly well for competitive advantage. For now, let's consider the example of an omnichannel business, the Commonwealth Bank of Australia (CBA), which leveraged its platform to become the tenth-largest bank in the world (by capitalization).[19] The bank has 51,700 employees and 1,380 branches and provides internet banking services to over 5.8 million active digital customers.[20] As with most financial services organizations, the bank's systems had evolved separately for different products, channels, and businesses. Depending on the product or channel, the staff needed to use multiple systems to check a customer's information—but these systems did not show all the products and services the customer used from all parts of the bank.

Over the last ten-plus years, CBA has built a series of platforms focused on improving customer service and reducing costs, including replacement of its core banking systems around 2008.[21] The bank began its platform journey by identifying the top twenty IT capabilities that its senior business executives believed they would need to compete in the future. These capabilities spanned IT infrastructure (e.g., networks, end-user computing, data centers, security), applications for the branch, online, financial, and core systems, processes (e.g., origination, service, back office, administrative), and data (e.g., customer, product, channel). The highest-priority capabilities at the time were those required to provide a consistent customer-service experience across different products, channels, and businesses. These capabilities included a single customer-data repository, a single CRM system, standardized service and sales processes, and the ability to track customer interactions across channels.

Four years after completing those upgrades in IT infrastructure, CBA delivered a set of platforms that not only improved its customers' experience and reduced the cost of supporting its operating model, but also enabled its lines of business to rapidly deliver new services.[22] This strategic approach to the investment and management of platforms has served CBA well. When it started this journey, many considered it a courageous move by the bank.[23] Today the investment and focus has paid off. Currently CBA is the largest bank in Australia by capitalization and the most successful in terms of annual profits and cost to income ratio.[24] CBA's investment in technology is regarded as critical to its success, and the bank's complete platform rebuild has played a significant role in its ability to be a leader in digital banking.

In 2015, CBA opened 950,000 new transaction accounts, with 12 percent of new accounts (which can be created in less than five minutes) opened through digital channels. Retail bank balances on those accounts were up 38 percent for the year. These developments were "absolutely dependent on the core platform," according to CEO Ian Narev. "Our view is really clear that the technology emphasis here is particularly showing through in customer preference in transaction banking."[25]

CBA has good financial products and a strong customer experience, but CBA's platform strategy has made the bank stand apart from the crowd.

## Your Business Model, Your Competitive Focus

We return now to our DBM framework and the four models for making money in the digital era: supplier, omnichannel, modular producer, and ecosystem driver. Combining the framework with the three sources of competitive advantage introduced in this chapter, we propose a starting point for where you need to build capability. If you haven't done so yet, go ahead and complete the self-assessment at the end of the chapter to determine how good your content, customer experience, and platforms are and which of these sources of competitive advantage will be the most important. And then let's see how those advantages fit in each of the four quadrants of the DBM framework (figure 3-2).

### *Supplier*

Suppliers sell through other companies. And even though suppliers may advertise directly to the end customers or engage with them on social media or use big data to understand their preferences, the customers are ultimately picking a product—hopefully theirs—through an intermediary. Therefore, suppliers compete for prominence with similar products, say, on supermarket shelves or in the minds of financial advisers.

FIGURE 3-2

## Sources of competitive advantage in next-generation enterprises

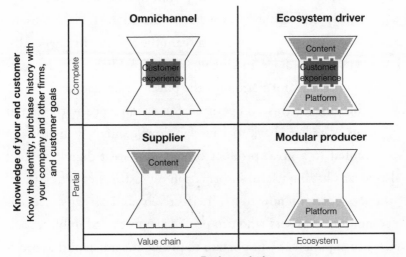

**Business design**
Who controls key decisions: brand, contracts, price,
quality, participants, IP and data
ownership, regulation

*Source:* © 2017 MIT Sloan Center for Information Systems Research. Used with permission.

To compete effectively, suppliers have to offer the best product for that customer's needs at that point in time. As importantly, they must have good access to the customer—the supermarket needs to display the supplier's products attractively or the financial adviser needs to fairly consider which supplier's products is a good fit for the customer's needs. Historically, this connection has led to all kinds of arrangements between suppliers and intermediaries. For example, mutual funds might pay up-front or trailing commissions to financial advisers. Digital—and to some extent, regulation—is leveling the playing field. A big leveler is search, which allows the end customer to find much more information about the fit of the product to his or her needs and to obtain similar customers' opinions, advice, and experiences. "Customers like me" are a great source of typically unbiased advice often sadly lacking in the traditional physical channels—populated with poorly trained shop servers or biased financial advisers. Sure, there are still many ways to scam the system. But generally, fellow customer advice and ratings are quite reliable and increasingly important information for the purchase decision.

So, because of this competition for prominence with similar offerings, suppliers have to have fabulous content, which is not just limited to a great product or service. Great digital content also means having useful information on features of the physical product, videos on how to use it effectively, and perhaps access to a community of users who can provide support and unbiased advice. For suppliers, it's important to provide as much of that product or service as digitally as possible. For physical products, that means digitizing the warranty registration process or automatically updating the operating system of a physical object, like a TV. For digital products, it means delivering the product immediately and keeping it up-to-date. Content is still king for suppliers.

## Omnichannel

Omnichannel businesses are more focused on meeting the customer's life-event needs and require significantly more customer intimacy than suppliers. However, we saw statistically few omnichannel businesses that were really great at customer experience. It's a big challenge to take a business designed for the physical world, add a digital channel, and make the new customer experience seamless. Most banks, energy companies, and formerly physical-only retailers are working hard on making the transition to omnichannel.

Executives at BBVA have thought long and hard about the mobile channel and concluded that the mobile phone should be the customer's remote control to the bank. This innovative concept allows the customers to be in control and use whatever channel they prefer, including getting assistance on that channel. For example, the mobile app enables a seamless live connection to the customer's remote relationship manager, a personalized appointment system, and fast tracking at the branch. In addition, for some BBVA products, customers can make digital purchases in less than a minute—and the bank is working to provide more products this way. The competitive advantage for an omnichannel lies in providing a great customer experience. Sure, any competitive advantage requires good products and good platforms, but the focus for omnichannel is customer experience. It also adds more intimacy to the customer-bank relationship—for example, in Spain the bank has said that it wants to make more than 90 percent of its products available to customers via their mobiles on a "do-it-yourself" basis by the end of the year. The result being customers are more engaged with the bank's mobile services because put simply they can do more with them—but that in turn allows the bank to interact more with those customers going forward.

## Modular Producer

The essence of the modular-producer model is the ability of the product or service to plug and play in anyone else's digital ecosystem. Modular-producer offerings have to be like LEGO blocks, with APIs that make it easy to connect to other enterprises' platforms. To be a modular producer, an enterprise must develop its products and services so that they operate in many countries and under various legal and compliance systems. Kabbage, a pioneer in providing working capital online to small-business owners, boasts more than one hundred thousand customers and $3 billion in small-business loans. The company offers an online source of funds in three easy steps that can take as little five minutes to complete: sign up, get an instant review with no paperwork, and withdraw funds up to $100,000. Kabbage uses its proprietary platform of analytics, relying on external data from multiple sources (including accounting information like QuickBooks, seller history, and social media) to make the loan approvals. The loans resemble a line of credit where customers pay only for what they need and use. This direct lending business will continue to grow, but in our view, Kabbage's great potential stems from its capacity as a modular producer.

In partnership with banks and other companies that have many small-business clients, Kabbage provides its instant working-capital loan service through another firm's ecosystem. Kabbage has recently announced partnerships with Santander UK, National Federation of Independent Businesses US, ING, and UPS. In these partnerships, Kabbage acts as modular producer in the partner's ecosystem of customers or members who need working capital. Through its success as a modular producer, Kabbage was ranked the thirty-sixth-fastest growing company on *Inc.*'s 5000 List in 2015.[26]

Kabbage and other modular producers must have world-class platforms. These platforms need to easily interconnect and operate in any enterprise's ecosystem in many countries. Just as important as all the data that modular producers handle, they need to learn and improve over time, while being fast and efficient. Modular-producer platforms tend to be algorithm heavy and data light. Like Kabbage, modular producers use data from many external sources, including the ecosystems with which they partner.

## *Ecosystem Driver*

The key to a successful ecosystem driver is to become *the first-choice destination* in a particular domain. Probably the most important decision for ecosystem drivers is deciding the domain. Amazon's domain has evolved from bookselling to general retail to a shopping destination that can provide almost everything a customer needs. 7-Eleven Japan, whose domain is convenience, is becoming the destination for solving the customer's daily needs. To make this goal a reality, a typical 7-Eleven Japan store has about three thousand products selected every few days by store clerks from a much larger set of products. To better meet their own daily needs, customers in the 7-Eleven store can access three million products across all the 7-Eleven parent company's brands—including department stores and supermarkets—through physical and digital channels. BMW, whose domain is transportation, wants to be your destination for tailored mobility, including buying or leasing a car or bike, renting a ride, and other forms of transportation.[27] Aetna's vision of "building a healthier world" means becoming the destination for your health-care needs. For Uber, it's about being your logistics destination by creating a digital net over a city—a net that includes personal transport, food delivery, and more services. All these companies have embraced ambitious, far-reaching visions to become the go-to destination in their chosen domain.

Being the destination in a chosen domain requires outstanding content, customer experience, and platforms. The combination of all three is what sets your enterprise apart and makes you *the* destination for customers. Ecosystem drivers typically not only sell their own great content but also offer complementary products as well as competitors' products that plug and play directly into their customer experience and platforms. The customer experience has to be best in class and constantly improving using the great data that ecosystems drivers collect. The platforms have to be double-sided—meaning that not only can customers use the platform but so can partners and competitors offering complementary products. For example, if you go to Vanguard.com and run your personal portfolio analysis, the tool might recommend reweighting your portfolio by increasing the percentage of bonds. The website will provide a list of bond funds that you can purchase. Naturally, Vanguard bond funds are the first suggested, but just a little further down, you'll see funds from competitors like Fidelity, USAA, Wells Fargo, and JPMorgan Chase. The platforms have to seamlessly provide all the information to the customer and then enable transactions without a glitch, whether you are buying a Vanguard fund or another brand.

The ecosystem driver is the only model that requires you to be world-class in all three competitive levers today—a very high bar that helps explain why there are so few successful ecosystem drivers. But let's look in depth at how one of those ecosystem drivers, LexisNexis, does it—competing daily on content, the customer experience, and platforms.

## LexisNexis: Strong Content, Customer Experience, and Platform

LexisNexis, one of the world's largest providers of information and analytics to the legal market, illustrates how one enterprise tackled the challenge of adapting and strengthening its digital competitive advantage. With 2016 revenues of $1.2 billion, LexisNexis has customers in about 130 countries with almost

100 percent market penetration in the large law segment and has billions of searchable documents. In 2016, the firm's operating margin was 19.2 percent, significantly outperforming the industry average of 4.6 percent. The operating environment at LexisNexis has become increasingly digital; its parent company, Reed Elsevier, reports that LexisNexis's total enterprise revenues from electronic content and tools increased from 22 percent in 2000 to 82 percent in 2016. Leaders at LexisNexis expect that this proportion will rise to almost 100 percent in the near future.[28]

As legal content has become more digitized, it has also become more commoditized. Search engines such as Bing and Google have gained importance as sources of information like contact details for lawyers, public records, and case law. Governments are also digitizing more of their public records, making them searchable and easier to obtain. In the domain of legal research, LexisNexis is one of three or four major players. How did it go about becoming *the* destination for its business customers—a place its customers find so valuable they won't switch legal research providers? Given the company's goal of becoming a 100 percent digital business, the answer was that LexisNexis strove to develop all three sources of competitive advantage to be best in class. It invested in more exclusive content, improved the multiproduct customer experience, and built a more flexible global platform.

## Creating Unique Content

LexisNexis has diversified its content to make it more valuable to lawyers. The firm continues to deliver public-record and case-law information in increasingly easy-to-find ways. But to create unique content, LexisNexis has developed relationships with top experts—celebrity lawyers—who provide opinions and commentary in many areas such as intellectual property, bankruptcy, constitutional, and tax law. These commentaries are updated regularly and enthusiastically received by lawyers practicing in each specialty. LexisNexis is growing user-generated content in other ways. It has agreements with several top law firms in the United States to generate expert commentary that is syndicated via LexisNexis channels. And it has built relationships with the some of the top legal bloggers in America. Common to all these efforts is the creation of unique content unavailable through any other source.

## Improving and Measuring the Customer Experience

LexisNexis has invested heavily in improving its customer experience. Market research based on focus groups and surveys is not getting the job done anymore, so LexisNexis assembled a team of anthropologists and sociologists to work closely with customers to identify unmet needs. The field researchers sit with clients and watch, asking them to describe the most frustrating parts of their day, observing the most frequently performed tasks, and generating ideas on how to better complete those tasks.

This deep customer-driven innovation has had big impacts at LexisNexis. For example, the field research helped change the product road map for the company's mobile efforts. The initial mobile strategy was to enable complete mobile access to all LexisNexis services. But the field research led to the insight that customers want to first perform quick, time-sensitive tasks on their mobile devices, like tracking time, looking up legal terms, and reviewing legal codes and precedents, each task via a dedicated app. LexisNexis has deployed a number of these targeted-task mobile apps with enthusiastic take-up by clients.

LexisNexis has also started implementing trackers at key customer touchpoints. These trackers, which assess satisfaction immediately, point out a problem before it can affect the customer's overall relationship with LexisNexis. The trackers also reduce the reliance on surveys, which have become annoyingly prevalent for us all. The efforts have paid off. In 2017, LexisNexis was awarded a Confirmit Achievement in Customer Excellence Award for its work on an internal tool that drives deep customer understanding across the system.[29]

## Developing a Flexible Global Platform

The LexisNexis global platform, Lexis Advance, was a complete refresh of the company's technology and processes. Among other elements, it enhanced the user experience and included features such as My Workspace (an online place to store, organize, and access legal research), better pre- and post-search filtering, visualization capabilities for research citation and verification, and new linking capabilities (e.g., case and codes can be linked to public records, company reports, verdicts, and more). The search capability encompasses the customer's content as well as LexisNexis and web content and provides results targeted to the user. The new platform was built for mobility so that data from the mobile apps will sync smoothly with the full-featured version. The platform was designed to both enable a great customer experience and empower a global content repository with exposed APIs to connect to client and partner systems. As a fundamental design principle, modularity encouraged both global and local innovation—enabling new capability to be easily added later.

The investments in digital capabilities, especially in mobile, provided LexisNexis customers a more seamless experience when they are moving from the office to the courtroom or client and back. Through its exclusive content, customers can access different viewpoints as they conduct their legal research. The global platform enables LexisNexis to provide these services at an affordable cost and to collect better data about its customers—what they do, when they do it, and where they are when they access the platform, either mobile or web. This data can be used to guide future innovations. While LexisNexis may not be the only destination in the domain of legal research, the improvements of all three sources of digital competitive advantage have helped drive the company's success.

As you consider the future importance of content, the customer experience, and platforms in your next-generation enterprise, you should consider a final question about budget and priorities. Which one or more of the three competitive advantages—content, experience, and platform—do you need to be a top-notch performer? And does your budget for next year reflect that prioritization? What would it take to change your budget priorities? Now is the time to strengthen your sources of digital competitive advantage as both your customers and your enterprise move from place to space.

This isn't always a fast or easy process, and coming to a consensus can be challenging. In a recent workshop with the top thirty partners and other leaders from a large law firm, we asked the participants to use the self-assessment tool at the end of this chapter. The results? Very strong, current-year scores across the group on content and relatively poor scores on customer experience and platforms. When asked to rank which of the three sources of competitive advantage would be most important for the firm's success three years from now, there was more difference of opinion, with some arguing quite eloquently for their position.

About half the participants—particularly participants with firmwide managerial responsibility—selected customer experience as the number one future source of competitive advantage. These leaders argued that, yes, they had good content and okay platforms, but most clients really wanted to solve their business life events (like starting operations in a new geographic location). These tasks required several parts of the law firm to cooperate on the legal services needed by their big corporate clients and to provide a more integrated customer experience.

About 40 percent of the participants chose content as number one, believing that their large corporate clients would continue to come to their law firm for the experts' opinions. They argued that corporate clients wanted to be confident about meeting with the best person and getting the best opinion for a particular matter. Therefore, content was still king, as were the expert lawyers.

The remaining 10 percent picked platforms; given that the big law industry was under serious threat, the business needed to transform. The leaders argued that the biggest threats were already coming from new law models that effectively use technology. The platform supporters believed they should invest and then lead in this area while the law firm was still in a strong position. It needed to build a strong digitized platform that automated much of the lower-value-added legal work like document review, enabling the top lawyers to add significant value. Platform leadership would allow the firm to respond to the pricing pressure from the new entrants and to react more quickly to client requests.

Honest conversations like these are critical for senior management teams in times of disruptive change. Otherwise, people are lulled into doing business as usual. For us, the experience at the law firm reinforced an essential truth: that knowledgeable people in the enterprise often disagree on important strategic issues and direction. Nevertheless, a discussion about the source of competitive advantage is a healthy and necessary conversation.

How about you? Where are your industry and your enterprise on this journey? If you haven't done so recently, now is a good time to review the sources of your digital competitive advantage.

In chapter 4, we'll look at what the internet of things and ubiquitous mobile devices and apps mean for your enterprise's path to digitization.

## Self-Assessment: Identifying Your Competitive Advantage

Where should you start? That depends on how good you are now and which capability will be most important for your enterprise's success in three years' time. The self-assessment will help you identify your digital competitive strengths and weaknesses.

Get as many colleagues as you can to self-assess your enterprise's current digital strengths and weaknesses, and identify which sources of competitive advantage—content, customer experience, or platforms—will be important in three years. Use the questions in the chapter 3 self-assessment, part 1, to stimulate discussion. Once you and your colleagues have discussed the three sources of competitive advantage, go to this chapter's self-assessment, part 2. Each person should first rate your enterprise's three sources of competitive advantage today, using a scale from 1 to 10. Then, average the scores across the group. Finally, each person should rank the importance of the three sources of competitive advantage for your enterprise in three years.

CHAPTER 3

## Self-assessment, part 1

### Questions to consider before beginning work on the self-assessment
### Content

- Do you continually add new or refreshed content to generate buzz in the marketplace?

- Of the content you provide today, what do your customers find most valuable? Do you have other internal content that could be provided to customers, for pay or for free?

- Who has responsibility for content in your enterprise? Is responsibility for digital products and information about physical products held by different groups? Should it be?

### Experience

- Do you know how good your customer experience is? Who owns it? What aspects of dealing with your enterprise do your customers like or find frustrating?

- How much of your revenue is generated online? How can you increase online cross-selling?

- How can you amplify the customer's voice to help continuously improve your customer experience?

- Who has the best customer experience in your industry among traditional competitors? Among new entrants?

- What changes, including organizational surgery, would it take to be the best customer experience in your domain?

### Platform

- How good are your internal digital platforms? Who owns them? Are they easy to use internally for innovating—i.e., can you quickly launch a new innovation using your existing platforms?

- How can you expose more of your internal digital platforms to your customers or partners to improve their experience?

- How can you better use external providers on your platforms—e.g., cloud, software as a service, partners, external data?

- How good are your partners' platforms? Can you link easily to those platforms?

*Source:* © 2017 MIT Sloan Center for Information Systems Research. Used with permission.

---

The average scores across the enterprises responding to our survey on their three sources of competitive advantage are 6.8 on the 10-point scale for content, 5.6 for customer experience, and 6.4 for platforms, with top-performing enterprises scoring 7.4 on content, 6.1 on experience, and 7.4 on platforms.[30] If your enterprise's scores on the questions are below average, your enterprise has some serious work to do.

CHAPTER 3

## Self-assessment, part 2

Rate your enterprise today on each of the three sources of competitive advantage (1 = Does not create business value, 10 = Creates significant business value)

Given the discussion in this chapter, rank—in the order of importance for success in your enterprise in three years—the three sources of competitive advantage (1 = Most important, 2 = Average importance, 3 = Least important)

**Today**        **In 3 Years**

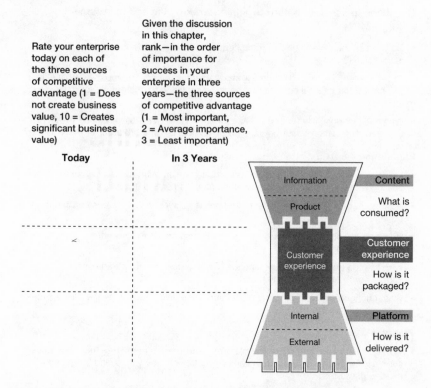

*Source:* © 2017 MIT Sloan Center for Information Systems Research. Used with permission.

Part 2 of this chapter's assessment could reveal disagreements about the direction your enterprise is heading. If you and colleagues differ on what your source of competitive advantage will be in three years, spend some time to try to move toward agreement. Once you've reached a consensus, you should aim to achieve the score of the top-performing firms in at least the one area you all agreed was the most important for success three years from now.

**CHAPTER 4**

# How Will You Connect Using Mobile and the Internet of Things?

More and more things in our world are acquiring digital sensors—from our pets and household systems to shipping containers and oil drills. Many enterprises are embedding those sensors in their products, although many executives don't exactly know how the companies will make money from the devices—yet.

Meanwhile, our mobile devices are capable of connecting to the internet of things (IoT) in myriad ways, turning our smartphones into remote controls for our lives. Not only can we employ mobile devices to manage the objects and systems we use, but those objects and systems can also use our devices to report to us regularly—while allowing manufacturers and other enterprises to keep tabs on their products and services centrally, creating better systemic outcomes. Simultaneously, an incalculable web of information expands, making that information available to an enormous number of other customers and enterprises.

The combination of mobile and the IoT changes everything, promising a level of knowledge sharing that we cannot yet fully begin to fathom. The big news? The intersection—the evolving use of mobile with the promise of the IoT—creates a powerful, high-value-added *overlap of interests*. The overlap offers a source of huge opportunity and financial gain for enterprise services and, for customers, enormous independence and control. Mobile plus the IoT is connectivity on steroids.

We came to that conclusion after more than five years of research on hundreds of companies as they moved their business models up and to the right on the DBM framework (toward becoming an ecosystem).[1] With the internal assets of the next-generation enterprise more easily connected, both control and innovation happen more easily. Connectivity is the essence of digitization and enables new business models we are only just beginning to discover.

As this potential win-win evolves both for customers and enterprises, the overlapping area between mobile and the IoT will no doubt become a battleground studded with more failures than successes. The potential—of both risks and benefits—of connectivity raises a question: How will your enterprise use mobile and digitally managed assets to connect and create the most value?

We partly answered that question in chapter 3 by exploring the enterprise's sources of competitive advantage—content, customer experience, and platforms. Technologies that connect enterprises and customers, like mobile and the IoT, become an important addition to your specific competitive advantage. For instance, IoT data, if used to create services, is content. Mobile is a terrific way to engage and connect to your customers, creating a better customer experience. Both mobile and the IoT can be put to use more powerfully when they are integrated into the platform.

This chapter takes the next step to help you, first, identify your mobile strategy and, second, examine how committed your enterprise is to the IoT. Finally, we'll help you find your sweet spot in the overlap between mobile and the IoT to create the most value for your business. Specifically, we will see significant consolidation among enterprises (mergers, acquisitions, etc.) as leaders in the use of these technologies dominate the ecosystem, gain connective power, and control more resources and as followers increasingly become commodity providers operating in the ecosystems of the leaders. Throughout the chapter, we draw on case studies from Dunkin' Donuts, Flex, GE, iGaranti, Johnson & Johnson, and Schindler to illustrate how to achieve connectivity and create value for your enterprise.

Let's start with mobile.

## What's Your Mobile Strategy?

It's hard to think of another technology more personally captivating than smartphones. This technology is personal and always with you, very engaging, and perhaps addictive (just look around you). Smartphones have sensors and cameras, keep track of location, can make payments, find information on anything, enable social connections, entertain you, are easily personalized—and integrate all those capabilities on a single, easy-to-use device.

As smartphones have advanced technologically and become ubiquitous, it's not surprising that mobile engagement has risen to

66 percent of our digitally connected time.[2] That's up from 2015, when American adults on average were on their mobile devices for 53 percent (174 minutes) of their daily total digitally engaged time. And that number already dwarfed the 2011 figure of 21 percent (42 minutes).[3]

With customers increasingly doing almost everything on their mobiles, enterprises need to find the best ways to engage people there. As yet, there's no proven one-size-fits-all model for how to do that, so it's up to individual enterprises to learn what works best while taking advantage of all that mobile has to offer. For digitally savvy people of any age, what was previously done with several enterprises on many channels over several days can now be done on a single mobile device in a few minutes.

Take, for example, booking a vacation. For most of us several years ago, booking a vacation was a multistep process taking several weeks and involving several channels and enterprises. We had to get ideas for great vacation spots, learn about the destination, find hotels, investigate airfares, and decide on a myriad of other details. We might need to make several visits to travel agents, go to consulates to get visas, and have many other interactions through both physical and digital channels.

Today everything you need to book that dream vacation—including reviews of hotels, exchange rates, the best deals on airfares, the ability to make payments, and even visa applications—is on your mobile device. And each of the previously separate enterprises that did a piece of your trip planning is vying to do more, or even all of it, to become your go-to enterprise for vacations. The result will be a consolidation of customer engagement into fewer go-to enterprises all brought together on a single mobile device in the hands of the customer. And this sort of ecosystem will be just as relevant for B2B enterprises. For example, Amazon Supply targets business customers with the same easy-to-use model that Amazon offers individuals, all from the mobile device. And it's true for banks as they work with institutional customers who want to see all their current positions, all their current accounts, and other information in a single place on the mobile device.

Besides consolidating services to become the go-to place for their mobile customers, enterprises can keep customers engaged by creating an app or a mobile-friendly website. Doing so can pay big dividends.[4] Pokémon Go, a highly engaging app innovatively mixing online interactions with real-world locations, achieved record levels of return visits and daily revenues of $1.6 million in its first week after launch in 2016.[5] Whether this level of profitability and engagement can be sustained is anyone's guess, but the app's fast success gives us a glimpse into the promise of augmented reality—and even more digital engagement.

And the stakes are high. In our global survey, the enterprises that achieved high customer-engagement goals via mobile also had net margins and revenue growth significantly higher than their industry average. To generate this premium, all enterprises need to develop their mobile customer-engaging muscle. As important as mobile apps and mobile-friendly websites are to enhancing an enterprise's current strategy, they can also help support an enterprise's internal organizational strategy—to reorganize around delivering great customer experience.

For example, earlier in the book, we introduced Garanti, Turkey's second-largest private bank (with a net margin of 39.2 percent—significantly higher than the 4.4 percent industry average—in 2016). When the bank decided to target new, young customers, it created iGaranti—a smart financial coach posing as a mobile app that addresses the everyday financial needs of millennials.[6] Some of the award-winning app's groundbreaking features include:

- Recognition of the customer's favorite brands, according to their spending patterns, and targeted and exclusive offers often based on GPS location

- Monthly budget estimates with warnings and advice regarding spending and potential shortfalls

- Social connections via Facebook and other social networks, and peer-to-peer money transfers

- Digital-wallet capabilities

- Drag-and-drop tiles to customize the app

- Voice input and output with a friendly avatar who listens and talks to the customer in natural language—no more typing!

Garanti found a way to reinvent banking for a new generation by moving from its traditional branch-based, product-centric strategy to one centered around mobile engagement. With record take-up from millennials, iGaranti will hopefully create a new generation of lifelong customers for the bank. The combination of data-rich interactions and a direct-to-the-customer channel allows Garanti to create and deliver offers that are more targeted and to build a tailored relationship with each millennial.

When thinking through how your own enterprise can similarly build the kind of mobile muscle to engage customers as iGaranti has done, remember that success depends not just on how much you spend, but also on how clearly you define your strategy and how effectively your organization executes it. In our research, we've identified five distinct mobile strategies you can use to build the kind of robust mobile applications that, when combined with the IoT, will move your enterprise toward becoming an eco-system driver. Here are the five strategies (in order of increasing potential impact on the bottom line):

1. **Brand enhancement:** Increase customer engagement by providing a useful, typically free, service that enhances the brand.

2. **Multichannel:** Improve the customer experience by integrating across channels.

3. **B2B2C:** Connect to end customers directly for enterprises that typically sell to end customers via another enterprise.

4. **Targeted segment:** Create a unique offering for an important segment.

5. **Mobile first:** Launch all innovations on the mobile channel.

Let's look at each of these strategies in turn.

## *Brand Enhancement*

A brand-enhancement mobile-app strategy aims to increase customer engagement with the brand. Enterprises have been very creative in how they use this strategy. Typically, the enterprise deploys a mobile app or website that is complementary to its products and services. For example, Johnson & Johnson, with more than 250 businesses, has several mobile apps designed to enhance its corporate brand. Here are a few such apps:

- **Care4Today Mobile Health Manager:** Supports and reminds user to stay on schedule with medications. Allows sharing of medication schedule with others.

- **Digital Health Scorecard:** Calculates a personal health score. Estimates the likelihood of developing common chronic diseases such as diabetes, heart or respiratory conditions, or cancer.

- **Donate a Photo:** For every user photo shared, Johnson & Johnson donates $1 to a cause the user supports.

- **J&J Official 7-Minute Workout:** Features a high-intensity aerobic and resistance-training session with video, tracking, and customization, using only the person's body weight and a chair.

Brand enhancement is a particularly attractive strategy for enterprises—often B2B enterprises—that want to make a first strategic entry into direct customer engagement through mobile but don't want to focus on selling their products or learning more about their customers. These enterprises are often suppliers that sell through intermediaries and want to move up on the DBM framework.

## *Multichannel*

A multichannel mobile strategy aims to enhance the overall relationship with the customer by providing a seamless cross-channel experience, better than either physical or digital channels alone. Woolworths is the largest retail enterprise in Australia, with three thousand stores and many brands spanning food, liquor, gas, and general merchandise. In 2016, the company had revenues of $42.4 billion and a net profit margin of 3.1 percent (compared with an industry average of 1.8 percent). Rather than target only online shoppers—whose purchases constitute just a fraction of its overall revenues—Woolworths launched a mobile app to enhance the shopping experience for all its customers with a smartphone.

The feature-laden app helps build a shopping list (e.g., by scanning bar codes), reorders the shopping list according to the aisle layout in the store a customer is visiting, highlights special offers that are based on customers' past loyalty-card purchases, and tracks fuel discounts. Shoppers who can't get to the store or who would rather buy online can press a single button to purchase all or part of their shopping list with same-day delivery in the major city areas. In a country of twenty-two million people, the Woolworths app has been downloaded more than two million times. The impact is impressive, with mobile-app users spending 65 percent more than physical-store-only shoppers spend. These numbers indicate that enhanced customer engagement on mobile apps can drive more total sales than does relying on the physical channel alone.

But success with mobile requires constant investment and innovation, and Woolworths has been struggling more recently as the retail market in Australia becomes more competitive with the strong performance of Aldi and other newer players, like Amazon.[7] The current competitive environment is an opportunity for Woolworths to build on its strong start with mobile to differentiate and further engage customers on their mobiles. For example, a new version of the app has many new features to increase engagement, like the ability to share family shopping lists, enhanced product searches, and notification when your favorite items are on sale.[8]

## B2B2C

In a B2B2C model, the enterprise historically hasn't connected directly with end customers, because it sells through another business. Using mobile apps, the enterprise can now make a real connection with the end customer. For example, P&G found that 83 percent of its customers decide before going to the store what product they want to buy.[9] Given that P&G historically rarely knew or connected directly with its 4.5 billion end customers, mobile apps and mobile-friendly websites are a chance to establish that connection. P&G began with websites like Pampers.com and now has mobile apps like Pampers Rewards—all designed to increase the customer's engagement with the brand and to influence the purchase decision.

The B2B2C model is also useful for franchise enterprises. As discussed in chapter 1, Dunkin' Brands, a successful franchisor of its fast-food restaurants worldwide, used a mobile app to better connect with its end Dunkin' Donuts customers. The DD Perks rewards program encouraged adoption of the app. The mobile app, in conjunction with DD Perks, gave the enterprise a much closer connection to the end customer and more insights into the Dunkin' Donuts customers' behavior. These sorts of B2B2C connections often offer benefits to both the enterprise and the end customer.

## Targeted Segment

Returning to our example of iGaranti, the Turkish bank's app was designed to target digital natives—people aged eighteen to twenty-eight—who live on their mobile devices. The goal was to attract young customers who had no banking relationship, slowly grow their portfolio of products and services by building strong engagement via the mobile app, and then make them loyal customers for life. The bank used a fresh design to create an emotional connection with the customer by making the app easy, social, proactive, and "cool." A money bar tracks spending patterns and then sends notifications and recommendations to the customer. The app has enjoyed strong engagement: 43 percent of customers who have ever logged in have become active users. And 10 percent of customers applied for a loan in their first year using the app.

## *Mobile First*

Westpac, one of the four large banks in Australia, views mobile as the front door to its organization, and its mobile-first strategy is a commitment to a new way of doing business. In 2014, with revenues of AUD$19.9 billion (US$18.3 billion), the bank declared that all new product and service offerings would be introduced in the mobile channel first. Westpac then delivered more than forty-five mobile and tablet apps across its four major brands. The bank's focus on mobile has generated impressive results. Within the first year, 7.5 percent of the enterprise's customers interacted with the bank by mobile only, and 20 percent of simple products—credit cards, simple loans, certificates of deposit, and the like—were sold on its mobile channel. Customers were clearly delighted: at the end of 2014, Westpac achieved a mobile net promoter score (NPS) of 63, compared with the average US bank's NPS of 34.[10] By the end of 2016, Westpac had revenues of AUD$26.8 billion (US$15.4 billion) and a net profit margin of 39.8 percent, and customers were still delighted, with 89.9 percent of them satisfied with Westpac's mobile banking.[11]

## Dealing with Challenges to Creating Great Mobile

Every enterprise needs to get great at mobile. But there are challenges. Here are actions you can take to ensure that your enterprise garners maximum impact from its customer mobile engagement:

- Decide which group in the enterprise is responsible for the customer experience—candidates include marketing, customer relationship management, IT, or a specific line of business. A great mobile strategy will often raise the question of which group is accountable for customers and will challenge the status quo of where power resides in your enterprise. If the question is not addressed, customers might receive different offers of mobile engagement from different parts of the company. Such lack of coordination may sound unlikely, but we see it all the time.

- Of the five mobile strategies, pick the one that is best for your enterprise. Set a high goal for increasing customer

A key strategic opportunity of mobile is the ability to capture very fast feedback from the customer and then effectively amplify the customer voice inside the enterprise. Mobile first is a significant strategic change requiring not only a commitment to mobile but also, typically, organizational surgery to realign the existing products and businesses so that mobile becomes the front door to the enterprise. For most enterprises, this realignment means engagement, and then execute on it. These practices will help you gain the confidence of senior management to support further customer engagement through mobile.

- Service-enable with APIs the essential transactional systems that make you great as an enterprise—your crown jewels. To create mobile apps or sites quickly, you need to separate the core transactions from the development of mobile apps or sites.

- Start the conversation of what a successful mobile strategy will mean for your other assets—your people and your physical enterprise. For example, for banks, retailers, universities, and enterprises that rely on a high-touch business model that is heavy on physical assets, mobile is likely to drive a different use of these channels (e.g., bank branches) and cause a slow and steady reduction in their use.

rethinking—and reorganizing—how the physical channels will be used in a mobile-first strategy.

---

Whatever strategy your enterprise chooses, developing your customers' mobile engagement can pay off handsomely. We found that 71 percent of the 334 enterprises we surveyed set high goals for mobile customer engagement, and the enterprises that achieved their high goals (43 percent of the 334 enterprises we surveyed) also had net margins and revenue growth of 5.5 and 6.1 percentage points, respectively, higher than their industry average. These top-performing enterprises set high goals, decided on a clear mobile strategy, and pursued that strategy to achieve their goals. We learned from our case studies that initial (often small) successes encourage more extensive use of the mobile channel to engage customers, accompanied by increasingly significant investments and organizational commitment. In the resulting virtuous circle, mobile-channel success spurs the enterprise to more and better mobile engagement with the customer.[12]

And as you reflect on the importance of mobile to your enterprise's overall strategy, consider the following questions: Is your business a leader or a follower when it comes to mobile? Is it achieving the kinds of bottom-line benefits we discussed in this section? Whose job in the enterprise is it to drive mobile success? And how can you energize the young people in your enterprise—who really get mobile—to help lead the charge? Your enterprise must answer such urgent questions before you can hope to move up in the DBM framework, toward ecosystem driver. For more on these issues, see the sidebar "Dealing with Challenges to Creating Great Mobile."

## How Strong Is Your Commitment to the IoT?

The IoT promises a connected world and new ways to delight customers and make money. This new landscape will change the way enterprises operate and engage with customers, suppliers, and partners. Essentially everything will be networked—products, people, and assets. The data created will be used to optimize both the demand and the supply side of the increasingly digital marketplace. Some enterprises will lead this process (and perhaps control their IoT networks), and others will be participants.

Whatever position your enterprise aims for in the IoT landscape, the stakes will be high. The coming IoT business market is estimated to generate up to $11.1 trillion by 2025.[13] Companies are investing $6 trillion globally in the IoT over the next five years, aiming to yield an estimated fifty billion IoT-connected devices by 2020 (with a 41 percent compound annual growth rate from 2016).[14]

These predictions have led to much lofty talk and strategic positioning. Our findings show that enterprises that succeed with an IoT strategy move their business models toward ecosystems (up and to the right on the DBM framework). How is this accomplished? For one thing, enterprises can create both top- and bottom-line value when they are willing to change their business models—for example, shifting from selling products to services—which is a major commitment to a new way of operating.

Technologically speaking, the IoT moves a business toward an ecosystem through the use of sensors and other Internet Protocol (IP)-enabled assets, connecting the network of physical objects to the enterprise and its own digital network. But the real power comes when enterprises can couple the IP-enabled assets with data analysis, algorithms, and other capabilities to respond automatically to customer needs—needs articulated by the customer as well as needs customers may not even know they have yet!

The next section examines different approaches to the IoT taken by three leading companies we have studied. But first, let's look at the main factor that ultimately will separate those who lead and prosper from those who follow in the coming hyperconnected world: a commitment to the IoT.

## *Commitment: The Ultimate Driver of Your Success in the IoT*

With the immense promise of the IoT, we wanted to understand how companies are using the IoT to change how they operate and the difference that can be observed thus far between the top and bottom performers. We suspect that the IoT is currently at the peak of the hype cycle. What typically follows next is the hard job of changing enterprises' business models to take advantage of the new opportunities, which can further widen the gulf between the top and bottom performers.

We surveyed 413 senior executives, asking about their IoT strategy and the results so far. Our findings? There is a strong relationship between the degree of enterprise *commitment* to the IoT and the generation of new business revenues.

Figure 4-1 starkly shows the contrast between manufacturing enterprises that have strongly committed to the IoT and those that haven't. There's a cluster of manufacturing enterprises at the top right of the chart. These enterprises have made a significant commitment to the IoT and generate between 60 and 90 percent of their revenues from new products or services introduced in the last three years. In contrast, the enterprises in the bottom left have a much lower commitment to the IoT and generate as little as 10 percent of their revenues from new products introduced in the last three years. The strong relationship between commitment to the IoT and the impact on revenues is striking—almost a straight line from bottom left to top right: the more commitment to the IoT, the higher the growth from innovation. We only show manufacturing firms for simplicity's sake, but the results were the same in all industries.

FIGURE 4-1

## Companies with greater commitment to the internet of things (IoT) have more growth from new products

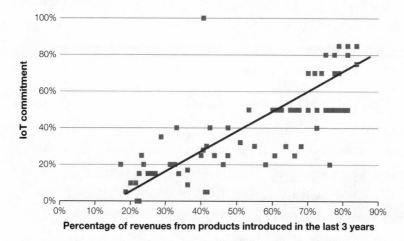

Source: MIT CISR 2015 CIO Digital Disruption Survey of 352 participants. © 2017 MIT Sloan Center for Information Systems Research. Used with permission.

What enables a company to commit to the IoT? We found the following four important components of such a commitment, which we will describe in more detail later in this chapter:

1. **Threat:** High threat from digital disruption spurred commitment to the IoT. Enterprises with numerous threats from digital disruption were more motivated to commit to the IoT as a growth or survival strategy.

2. **Vision:** Executive committee members spent more time analyzing and discussing digital disruption, and CIOs spent more time focusing their teams on innovation.

3. **New IoT capabilities:** Enterprises committed to the IoT had more open APIs for internal use and for external

enterprises to connect to than did companies less committed to the IoT.

4. **Organizational readiness:** Enterprises can commit to the IoT when they have more capabilities—leadership, investment, governance, sharing—to make the significant changes needed for shifting business models.

The impact of high commitment is spectacular. For enterprises in the top quartile of IoT commitment, 50 percent of their revenues on average came from new products introduced in the last three years. In contrast, enterprises in the bottom quartile of IoT commitment averaged only 16 percent of revenues from new products introduced in last three years.

At a recent workshop we conducted on the IoT for about forty-five CEOs, the difference between low and high commitment became very clear. A CEO of an energy enterprise told us, "Our goal is to design, invite participants to join, and lead an IoT network to deliver complete solutions to our customers." That CEO's high-level commitment is likely to lead the company toward becoming an ecosystem driver using the IoT as the technical vehicle. By contrast, the CEO of an enterprise that makes electrical motors said, "Our goal is to participate in as many IoT networks run by other enterprises as necessary to ensure our motors are connected everywhere"—a less ambitious goal that will probably make the business into a modular producer.

Of course, many companies will need to do both—act as an ecosystem driver and a modular producer. Most companies will try to lead at least one IoT network and participate in several networks led by other companies. For example, the energy company mentioned above will strive to lead an IoT network based on energy management but will also participate in several IoT networks led by other companies, perhaps construction companies or building-management companies. Whether to lead an IoT network, to participate in several networks led by others, or to do both is the key decision companies must make when they are formulating their IoT strategy.

## Three Company Journeys to the IoT

In the three cases that follow, you'll see that each enterprise focuses on one of those two goals. Flex is a supplier helping other companies build their IoT capabilities and move to the right on the DBM framework toward modular producer or even ecosystem driver. Schindler is a 140-year-old company that is becoming IoT-enabled to better serve its customers and move up and to the right on the framework, from supplier to omnichannel to ecosystem driver. Finally, GE is betting its entire enterprise on succeeding with the IoT by moving from an omnichannel model to becoming an ecosystem driver.

### *Flex*

Formerly known as Flextronics, Flex is a $24 billion revenue enterprise (as of 2016) that helps its customers create new products and solutions, bringing to life its IoT strategies by providing design, manufacturing, and supply-chain services.[15] CEO Mike McNamara explains, "The power of these end-connected nodes [machinery or other devices with sensors attached] is they are alive in the environment, collecting and reacting to environmental data, adapting to the information that's in the environment and adjusting in real time. The business model is then built around the data and the information. But you need hardware to connect and get the data." Flex's commitment to the IoT is demonstrated in the four components we identified as critical to IoT success.

**Threat.** Flex's traditional business, contract manufacturing, was successful but had slim margins and attracted low-cost competitors.[16] Flex observed that many of its customers and other enterprises were facing quicker technology-innovation cycles, shorter product lives, and a huge demand for technology-enabled offerings like connected products.

**Vision.** To meet the growing need of enterprises that want to create connected products, Flex launched its Sketch to Scale strategy, a service relying on modular capabilities that could be used as building blocks for any hardware product. Former chief marketing officer Michael Mendenhall says, "Most enterprises understand that they can't achieve that velocity on their own. We cultivate their innovation and verify, test, and certify. We make the innovation highly reliable, and build through the commercialization process, even tax and trade, getting enterprises to market quicker."

**IoT capabilities.** To make Sketch to Scale real and deliver customers' products as quickly as possible, Flex identified seven core enabling technologies for the IoT and created a center of excellence (a group of people with skills focused on a specific area) for each.[17] These seven technologies also represent a good list of the core capabilities any enterprise should have in place for its IoT strategy:

- Sensors and actuators

- Security and computing

- Human–machine interface

- Connectivity

- Smart software

- Battery and power

- Flexible technologies and miniaturization

Flex can help a client in any market (from digital health to wearable sports technologies) go from "sketch to scale" by taking several of the preceding capabilities from its centers of excellence, connecting them, and creating a customized product.

**Organizational readiness.** Flex consolidated its design engineers with expertise in innovation into one organization to increase cross-industry learning. In addition, it established a high-level role to oversee all innovation. When the new IoT design and services created a demand for more partnering, both internally and externally, Flex developed better partnering capabilities. Finally, Flex designed a four-stage innovation process to help move its customers from ideation to commercialization (part of its Sketch to Scale strategy).

Today Flex works in relationships with clients like Nike, Ford, and Johnson & Johnson—with impressive results. Flex technology can be found in 85 percent of wearable sports technologies, and the firm is now developing more than 130 reusable components.

## The Schindler Group

Schindler manufactures, installs, and maintains escalators, elevators, and moving walkways.[18] The group is active in one hundred countries with over fifty-eight thousand employees and 2016 revenues of US$9.5 billion, with above-industry-average return on assets. Regularly recognized as one of the world's most innovative enterprises, Schindler has addressed the four important components of an enterprise's commitment to the IoT.[19] Let's consider them one by one.

**Threat.** The elevators and other products that Schindler makes are sold in an increasingly price-sensitive market. Constant innovation is demanded in the Asian growth market, where 60 percent of new installations occur. Maintenance accounts for 50 percent of industry revenues and about 75 percent of operating profits. Local enterprises that didn't install the elevator can provide maintenance services, typically competing strongly on price and potentially luring customers away from Schindler.

**Vision.** Over the last decade, Schindler has transformed its vision from being a product-focused engineering enterprise to a customer-oriented service provider. The company's goal is to outperform competitors in an increasingly price-sensitive market through cost leadership and service. Schindler combines several digital technologies such as sensors and mobile technologies, coupling them with analytics, to enable a global proactive and predictive service model.

The firm has also focused on several business-model changes. It now provides a whole new level of optimized services built around service technicians. The enterprise is also working on better elevator and escalator products. And Schindler now provides a great customer experience through apps that combine data from sensor-enabled equipment and Schindler's responses.

**New IoT capabilities.** Schindler's new capabilities include sensors on elevators that send more than two hundred million messages a day on elevator performance; a business-rules engine and predictive analytics to analyze sensor data and then take action; and a customer web portal and mySchindler app to provide real-time information to customers and service technicians.

The sensors, which can collect as many as 750 to 1,000 points of data from an elevator, are now deployed on the vast majority of new lifts, and the enterprise is retrofitting old lifts with the technology. Schindler is using this data first to learn about impacts on the elevator environment, such as temperature, and then to enhance elevator and escalator products using the information. In addition, complex algorithms in the business-rules engine apply sensor data to predict equipment problems, including failure, and the demand for spare parts. Schindler has also invested heavily in the passenger experience with its PORT Technology, which decreases passenger wait times by applying authentication and smart algorithms to optimize elevator routes. This type of service helps customers that run facilities to differentiate themselves. In large buildings, Schindler anticipates managing the efficient flow of up to thirty thousand people at morning and evening peak times.[20]

**Organizational readiness.** To facilitate increased digital innovation and move toward implementing their new business model, Schindler made several changes, both organizational and technological. First, it brought together its digital capability into one unit—Schindler Digital Business AG, which was created in 2013. This move combined several parts of the enterprise, including R&D, IT, service and installation, industrial design, and gaming. Schindler also created a matrix organization across many functional groups for knowledge sharing and synergies and developed a global business platform called SHAPE (Schindler Harmonized

Applications for Process Excellence) to make sense of data available across all business processes.

Another change at Schindler occurred when it started involving users directly in the design of solutions—a technique widely used in startups. Finally, the company began focusing on rapid innovation to create a minimal viable product. Rather than offering customers a complete solution with many options and hence takes longer to produce and evaluate, a minimum viable product has only the necessary core features. Once the minimum viable product is deployed, the company gathers feedback about the product from early adopters, using that information to build a final product that most customers will want.[21]

## *GE*

This American conglomerate is an interesting example of an enterprise whose goal has been to lead an IoT network, as opposed to being a participant. Several years ago, the previous CEO of GE, Jeff Immelt, announced a major change in strategy: to help create and manage the "industrial internet." One of us (PW) was in a roomful of senior leaders when Immelt described this new vision—and the reaction was awe and admiration for its boldness. Many changes followed, all of which contribute to GE's commitment to the IoT.

**Threat.** GE's stock price tumbled during the 2008 financial crisis and has not recovered. Moreover, it has significantly underperformed the S&P 500.[22] Growth has been sluggish, with a five-year revenue growth rate of –3.3 percent.[23]

**Vision.** Immelt articulated a vision: industrial engineering and manufacturing combined with big-data analytics. It wasn't enough to build industrial machines. Those machines had to be connected and the data collected and analyzed to improve performance. This vision harkens back to GE's roots in heavy industry and industrial automation.[24]

**IoT capabilities readiness.** GE created a software business and an IoT platform called Predix, built to support GE's use of the "industrial internet."[25] With Predix, GE can capture, store, and analyze data and make it available to enterprises to make decisions and monitor their businesses.

**Organizational readiness.** GE is focusing on its vision and making organizational changes to support that vision. The company sold its GE Capital Assets division in 2015 and its appliance division in 2016.[26] Up for selling consideration now is its lighting division.[27] In its search for new software and technical talent, GE moved its headquarters to Boston to be near world-class technology and education.[28]

Although today only 3 percent of industrial data is tagged and used productively, GE expects global investment in the so-called industrial IoT to grow dramatically. When that time comes, Predix will be ready to securely connect with any IP-enabled machine, both GE-made and non-GE-made.

GE positions Predix as a way to offer internal GE businesses and clients "connectivity as a service." It will grow its industrial-internet-management business first for internal GE businesses, like airline engines and oil and gas. Later it will manage clients' IoT-based businesses. That's how GE is both leading an IoT network for its own businesses and offering those services to clients to enable their IoT-based businesses.

This approach is not unlike Amazon's business model around AWS (Amazon Web Services), a cloud-computing service. Amazon uses AWS technology capability for its own businesses and provides the further capacity to clients to generate Amazon revenue and subsidize its infrastructure costs. For GE clients, GE Digital explains, "Predix microservices are reusable software modules that can be leveraged as building blocks to rapidly create applications."[29] It's a bold vision for GE's growth strategy, using the platform for its own traditional businesses and to create new revenue streams by helping clients enable their own IoT-based visions.

---

Return now to the DBM framework, keeping in mind the examples we've just described—GE, Schindler, and Flex. GE's vision for Predix as an enabler of its own and others' businesses and Schindler's vision to provide seamless elevator and other urban mobility solutions exemplify enterprises aspiring to lead an IoT network and become ecosystem drivers. On the other hand, enterprises such as Flex, which have connectable assets but aren't leading an IoT network, will be participants in an IoT network led by another enterprise. Enterprises like these will become modular producers, with all this model's joys and frustrations. If your enterprise is a modular-producer leader, you are in an enviable position—great market share will lead to nice profits. Unfortunately, if you are way down on the market-share totem pole, then it's a race to the bottom.

## A Powerful Combination: Mobile and the IoT

Our examination in this chapter so far—first of the growing mobile landscape and then of the promise of the IoT—brings us to perhaps the most powerful opportunity for the next-generation enterprise: a world of mobile-only customers coupled with expansive IoT network strategy. Such a combination creates a formidable team for creating value, especially when used to move up and to the right on our DBM framework.

The intersection of mobile and the IoT immediately puts customers in control by letting them use their mobile devices to identify the services, people, assets, and apps they want to connect with and manage. Enterprises can provide solutions to customer needs through a set of services coordinated by an IoT-enabled network. Competitive advantages will then go to enterprises that see and act on the much-improved data they'll have about their customer actions and by learning how their products are used.

Many interactions will be automated, with enterprises engaging a customer through mobile and, with prior permission, using an algorithm to act. For example, if your home security is breached, the system will take action with cameras, sirens, alarms, lights, locks, and so on. And soon, enterprises will be able to do more-complex analysis, like minimizing home energy use or maximizing crop yields, and generally will see much better data about what their customers want and how their products are used. And through partnerships, they will provide a much broader set of services. Customers will also get much better data about how their needs are met now and what the available options are. Moreover, business customers will have a single place to manage energy, transportation, or legal or pricing information.

The high-value-added overlap between customers and enterprises will become the strategic battleground for enterprises in the near future, leaving some enterprises behind. If an enterprise can both lead an IoT network and engage customers for most of their needs through their mobile devices, the result will be strong growth and increasing dominance.

For example, who will lead the IoT network in your smart home? Enterprises are already waging a battle over that territory. For example, Philips and Flux manufacture IoT-enabled lightbulbs, Motorola and Belkin produce connected cameras, and Honeywell and Nest enable IoT-connected environmental management. There are IoT-enabled locks by Schlage and August and IoT televisions by Sony and Vizio, and IoT-enabled everything else is on the way.

Which enterprise will you trust to coordinate all those assets and the associated data from a single app on your mobile device? That enterprise will have tremendous power in the IoT network and will have access to your data. Notice in each of the preceding examples, there is a traditional player and a new entrant vying for leadership. That is the essence of more digital disruption. It's no surprise that Apple has announced Apple HomeKit to coordinate your smart home. But what about Amazon Alexa and ADT and AT&T and the many others? All these enterprises are vying to be the controller of your smart home.

This profusion of data will lead to many conversations about privacy and companies' acceptable use of data.[30] The topic of digital privacy merits its own book, but we'd like to make a couple of observations. For the customer, the digital world is a trade-off between our own sense of privacy and how much data we are willing to share to get better services, more convenience, and lower cost. For companies, it's all about how they get the most value from the data without crossing the creepiness line—and this requires building company norms around acceptable data use.[31] And of course, the creepiness line is moving as most of us get more used to the idea of our data being seen by service providers.

Enterprises will have to take the lead in building norms of acceptable data use. Here are some practices that can help your enterprise:

- Check how you use data—do your practices make you cringe?

- Make sure you are providing value to customers in exchange for the data.

- Tell stories that show how individuals are affected by the use of their data—are there positive impacts?[32]

To help us begin to explore those implications and more, we return to the DBM framework. What will determine success in the highly connected next-generation enterprise? And where in the overlap of IoT and mobile might your company find its sweet spot?

## The DBM Framework: Bringing All the Pieces Together

As we examine what it takes to succeed in a mobile-only and IoT world, let's return to our DBM framework for the next-generation enterprise. For example, if you decide to use Apple HomeKit in your home, Apple will become the ecosystems driver for your home, and the providers of the connected, non-Apple devices will be acting as modular producers.

Going one step further, we combine the two IoT strategies described earlier—leading an IoT network versus participating in several IoT networks led by others—with the five mobile strategies outlined at the beginning of the chapter: brand enhancement, B2B2C, multichannel, targeted segment, and mobile first.

Now, let's look again at mobile devices. We envision the customer doing almost everything from the mobile device—inside a mobile app or mobile-friendly web environment. A mobile app designed to be used only on an Apple, a Samsung, or another device provides an attractive "walled garden" that's easy to use, customizable, integrated, socially connected, and secure, and it relies on the camera and sensors of the ever-more-sophisticated mobile device. Mobile devices will become easier to use and more powerful; they will have better connectivity and more sensors. A responsive website, on the other hand, is device agnostic, though it may not be able to use the capabilities of the mobile device to the fullest and is likely less sticky than a successful app. The interesting questions will be whether a mobile app is the best way to meet life-event needs (either B2B or B2C). Can one mobile app or responsive website cover most of such needs? Or will it be a different ecosystem-driver app or website in each of several domains, such as Amazon for customer products, Fidelity for wealth management, Aetna for health care, and Netflix for entertainment? For B2B, what does the list of companies offering to meet enterprise life events look like? Will it be Salesforce for managing customers, SAP for managing operations, BNY Mellon for providing financial services, Bloomberg for delivering enterprise information, and Alibaba for business purchasing?

Enterprises have an important strategic choice to make. Should, and can, your enterprise lead an IoT network? Or should it participate in one or more IoT networks led by other enterprises? Or should it perhaps pursue both strategies in different markets or segments?

Take Schneider Electric. The IoT is critical to Schneider Electric's move toward its mission of leading the digital transformation of energy management and automation. The company could lead an IoT network for energy management—acting as an ecosystem driver—that includes customers, partners, products, assets, data, and services. Schneider Electric would also determine who could participate and under what conditions. At the same time, the company could sell its products or services to other enterprises that want to lead their own IoT networks. Under these circumstances, Schneider Electric would be a modular producer.

There is a high-value-added zone in the future, where the customer needs and enterprise services overlap. In this zone, the customer is in control but the enterprise profits through sales of products and services and the collection of valuable data. The customers can set conditions about when and how they want to buy services and automate those decisions if they choose. At the simple end of this continuum, you can imagine the automatic ordering of household goods when inventories are low. In a more sophisticated future, an enterprise or network could monitor all the equipment in a customer's house (or office or factory), manage energy consumption, order maintenance, and even purchase replacements. The possibilities are virtually endless. This is the sweet spot where you want your company to be. So how do you use what we've explained about mobile and the IoT to land in that spot? With that question in mind, let's look at the DBM framework again.

## Ecosystem Drivers

In a DBM nirvana for ecosystem drivers, an enterprise leads its own branded IoT network, recruits numerous other enterprises to be participants, and controls the key decisions about brand, contracts, how prices are set, how quality is assessed, who owns the intellectual property, and, most importantly, who owns and sees what data. For those potential benefits, it will have to take on the accountability for regulation, compliance, security, and other coordination efforts. In addition, the big cost will be the up-front investment in developing the branded IoT network and recruiting participants, and this investment may or may not take off. At the same time, the ecosystem driver needs to have a great mobile-first strategy for its customers. The ecosystem driver aims, through its IoT network, to be the destination of choice for customers who are using their mobile devices and the enterprise-branded app or website to access everything they need within the domain specified by the ecosystem driver—whether it be health care, entertainment, financial services, corporate advisory, technology solutions, or something else.

## Omnichannels

The omnichannel enterprise seeks to provide service for their customers' needs on whatever channel the customers choose. Like the Spanish bank BBVA, more enterprises are likely to adopt the idea of the mobile device as a remote control for the customer's engagement with them, using a multichannel mobile strategy. The minimum requirement from an IoT perspective will be to participate in any relevant IoT networks. For example, in the insurance industry, IoT networks could connect assets like cars, houses, buildings, and boats and share information to more accurately price insurance policies and manage claims. Customers could more easily gather insurance quotes from their devices and make decisions. We may even see customers able to disaggregate their policies to get the best deal for each of their major assets. At the minimum, an insurance enterprise will need to participate in those IoT networks led by others. But a grander vision may emerge from some insurance or financial services enterprises—a vision in which they aspire to be the leader of a branded IoT network.

There are pros and cons to the question of whether the leader of the branded IoT network for an industry like insurance should be an insurance enterprise or another enterprise like a shared utility. This debate is very similar to the one about computer reservation systems (CRSs) in the airline industry thirty years ago. Once it became clear that these systems were going to be very powerful, enterprises like United Airlines and American Airlines, which had developed great CRSs, spun them off into independent businesses with more-complex ownership or governance structures to enable the participation of competitors and complementors.

## *Suppliers*

The high-value-added overlap between mobile and the IoT is yet another dilemma for suppliers but also a significant opportunity. Most suppliers will need to move up the vertical axis of the DBM framework to better understand their end customers. A mobile strategy starting with brand enhancement (e.g., Johnson & Johnson) and then evolving to a B2B2C (e.g., Dunkin' Donuts) is a great model for success. By definition, a supplier is likely to have to participate in many IoT networks. But which networks will be the most successful for the supplier? Will they be run by their traditional customers (like Carrefour, Sainsbury, or Walmart for Johnson & Johnson), or will it be newer customers like Amazon or Alibaba or even a yet-to-be-created entity who are leading an IoT network? At this point, we can only speculate, but suppliers will need to be able to participate in multiple and sometimes competing IoT networks, while at the same time giving their customers a mobile way to interact with them.

## Modular Producers

For modular producers, mobile strategies present an interesting dilemma. For example, PayPal has a mobile app, but many people typically only use the mobile app to look at their account if there's a problem. The frequent transactions for payments enabled by PayPal operating as a modular producer are typically done at the virtual checkout of an enterprise that uses PayPal's payment services. Therefore, PayPal and other modular producers will need a mobile engagement strategy for a targeted segment to delight the frequent PayPal users who want to manage their payments through a mobile app. This segment is perhaps the best group of customers for which PayPal can aspire to become more of an ecosystem driver by providing additional services. A modular producer needs to operate easily in any other ecosystem, and doing so includes participating in many IoT networks. When a leader of a branded IoT network needs a payment service, as it most likely will, PayPal and its competitors will need to be plug-and-play compatible with that network.

Throughout this chapter, we have explored how the concurrent, dramatic rise of both mobile and the IoT presents a tremendous opportunity for enterprises to improve their strategic positions (or carries the risk of weakening their positions). Take the assessment at the end of the chapter to see how you compare with top performers on your mobile and IoT capabilities.

Moreover, as we saw in our statistical analysis of both mobile and IoT success, the stakes are high, with leaders and followers quickly established. The safe strategy is to do experiments to identify future business opportunities for your enterprise's success in all four quadrants of the DBM framework, incorporating a mobile and IoT strategy. The more ambitious and risky option—such as the one GE is pursuing—is to recognize that the world is changing fast and that your enterprise will be a fundamentally different enterprise in a decade if it's going to thrive.

In the next chapter, we turn our attention to building specific capabilities that will help your business move up and to the right on the DBM framework for the next-generation enterprise.

## Self-Assessment

How ready is your own enterprise to take advantage of mobile and the IoT to move up and to the right on the DBM framework? Take the chapter 4 self-assessment to see how your enterprise compares on mobile readiness and its commitment to the IoT. The average scores across many enterprises are 30 on the 50-point scale for mobile readiness and 18 for IoT commitment, with top-margin enterprises scoring 35 on mobile readiness and 29 on IoT commitment.[33] If your enterprise is planning to take advantage of both mobile and the IoT, its scores should be above average on both parts of the assessment. If your scores are average or below, evaluate whether you have the capabilities in-house to increase your mobile muscle and your commitment to the IoT. Many of the companies we have observed in their transformation use partners to move fast, gain access to skills, and build capabilities. How fast do you need to move?

# Self-assessment

## Mobile Readiness

To what extent is your senior management involved in your enterprise's mobile initiatives? (1 = Not at all, 10 = Very involved)

☐

To what extent are customers involved in your mobile design and development efforts? (1 = Not at all, 10 = Very involved)

☐

What percentage of your revenues comes from the mobile channel? (1 = None, 10 = All of them)

☐

To what extent does your mobile initiative use API-enabled enterprise capabilities? (1 = Not at all, 10 = We rely on APIs)

☐

To what extent are you capturing and using customer data from your mobile initiatives? (1 = Not at all, 10 = We capture and use all the data)

☐

**Total (out of 50)**

## IoT Commitment

How important to your enterprise success is a well-developed IoT initiative? (1 = Not important, 10 = Critical to our success)

☐

What percentage of your assets are IP-addressable now? (1 = None, 10 = Most of them)

☐

How involved is your CIO in your enterprise's innovation initiatives? (1 = Not at all involved, 10 = Critical to the success of all our innovation efforts)

☐

How involved is your executive team in developing the digital strategy? (1 = Not at all involved, 10 = Critical to the development of the strategy)

☐

How ready is your organization to change to take advantage of IoT? (1 = Not at all ready, 10 = Very ready)

☐

**Total (out of 50)**

*Source:* © 2017 MIT Sloan Center for Information Systems Research.

*Note: API* = application programming interface; IoT = internet of things.

## CHAPTER 5

# Do You Have the Crucial Capabilities to Reinvent the Enterprise?

What is your primary domain in the market, and how will you re-invent the enterprise to become the go-to choice in your domain? That's the question we've posed in various forms throughout this book because, simply put, enterprises will not survive the digital economy without reinventing themselves. Leaders must teach their lumbering elephants to dance.[1]

Reinvention requires a compelling vision that enables an enterprise to offer the best customer experience while also being agile, efficient, innovative, and great places to work for and to do business with. A tall order, perhaps. But the alternative is allowing startups and savvy large enterprises to slice and dice your company with their enticing, digitally enabled business models.[2]

## Schneider Electric Reinvents Itself

As described in previous chapters, in 2009 Schneider Electric made the transition from selling products to offering products and services, a change program the company called "One Schneider." Essentially, Schneider Electric, then nearly 175 years old, changed its self-description from a "manufacturer and distributor of electrical products" (a supplier) to a "provider of intelligent energy management and automation solutions" (an ecosystem driver). The company changed how it engaged with customers by designing customer journeys for its business units, a way to guide the units in more digital customer interactions. It also designed mobile apps and websites that allow users to plan their own product specifications. Today, the mySchneider app gives customers access to support 24/7 and lets them tailor alerts and download documentation.

To achieve this new compelling customer offer, Schneider Electric made a series of investments (buying options) that laid the groundwork for change, and it followed up with some major organizational surgery to cement the changes. Following the successful One Schneider program in 2009, Schneider Electric completed another three-year company program, from 2012 to 2014, called Connect.[a] The goal of Connect was to foster a highly collaborative, connected enterprise across business units and geographic locations. To enable Connect, Hervé Coureil, then–executive vice president of information systems, transformed the IT organization from a centralized provider of IT services to an orchestrator with the stated ambition of "digitized to empower." Schneider Electric reinvented the role of the IT organization to provide standardized

APIs (application programming interfaces) to be consumed by all the businesses. The service-enabled APIs of Schneider Electric's core capabilities are part of what makes the enterprise great (in Schneider Electric's case, energy management and automation products and services) and make the products and services available for easy use internally and externally. Connect's goal was to link customer-facing employees to the service-provision part of Schneider Electric seamlessly and securely.

Enterprises are often good—at any one point in time—at either cost savings or innovation, but rarely are they good at both. Companies tend to go through expansive times of innovation and growth but then need to tighten their belts and cut costs for a year or two or more. The top-performing enterprises in the digital era are "ambidextrous" in a sense—simultaneously innovating and cutting costs while often using the money saved with one hand to feed the innovation done with the other hand. Schneider Electric's leaders, while innovating the value proposition and cross-selling to the customer, were also making the enterprise more efficient. For example, they created a new global supply chain with centralized procurement, manufacturing, and distribution, and global functional support organizations such as finance, IT, and HR. In the past, Schneider Electric had had numerous local, autonomous IT organizations, each with its own data, processes, and systems. The global CIO had to coordinate more than fifty local IT leaders across Schneider Electric. The creation of the Information, Processes and Organization (IPO) standardized and reduced costs. The creation of the function was a huge change and not without its challenges, but the consolidation continues to reap benefits and is recognized industry-wide. For instance, in 2016, Schneider Electric jumped 16 places to number 18 in the Gartner 2016 Supply Chain Top 25 ranking.[b]

But Schneider Electric's organizational transformation went beyond building the global supply chain and consolidating the functional support organizations. Schneider Electric also created a new organizational design, with four guiding principles. First, overall profit-and-loss ownership and resource-allocation decisions would be organized by business. Second, customer-facing operations would be organized by country. Third, global supply-chain management would be centrally organized by function—procurement, manufacturing, and distribution as well as global functional support organizations such as finance, HR, and IT. And finally, specific global businesses would be created to handle all the global go-to-market models (such as global accounts, software, or digital services). All these organizational changes supported the new business model and reinforced Schneider Electric's competitive advantage.

a. Schneider Electric, "Connect: Company Program for 2012–2014," press release, Schneider Electric, February 22, 2012, http://www2.schneider-electric.com/documents/presentation/en/local/2012/02/20120222_Our-new-company-program_EN.pdf.

b. "Schneider Electric named to Gartner's Supply Chain Top 25 Ranking for the First Time," Schneider Electric press release, May 26, 2016, https://www.prnewswire.com/news-releases/schneider-electric-named-to-gartners-supply-chain-top-25-ranking-for-first-time-300275645.html.

In this chapter, we address how an enterprise makes the transition and reinvents itself into a more successful business model, according to our DBM framework. Namely, enterprise leaders decide which experiments—business model, structures, skills, and practices—they need to invest in and develop for the future. To successfully learn from those experiments, an enterprise must succeed at two strategic tasks:

1. Building a digital culture and structure—the shared values, beliefs, traditions, and assumptions about digital that guide behaviors

2. Becoming ambidextrous by simultaneously innovating and cutting costs

See the sidebar "Schneider Electric Reinvents Itself," which describes how the company created options for the future to accomplish these tasks.

In this chapter, we recount two stories that vividly remind us why enterprises cannot delay reinvention. One story describes a customer experience with a company caught frozen in the headlights of incompletely executed digitization; the other describes a company that has taken the digitization opportunity and run with it, picking off customers from larger companies (banks, in this case) along the way. Next, we draw on those stories and other company examples to examine eight organizational capabilities that enterprises master when they successfully navigate digital reinvention. We offer a self-assessment to determine where your enterprise stands regarding the eight capabilities, how it compares with other surveyed companies, and where it should focus for reinvention. Finally, we return to the example of BBVA to address some questions we often hear in our workshops: How do you set the vision for reinvention? And how do you change the culture?

# Why Enterprises Need to Reinvent Themselves for Digitization

The following two stories highlight why enterprises cannot delay reinvention in the digital age. They illustrate how a large, older enterprise will need to reinvent itself if it stands a chance of meeting the challenges presented by new, digitally enabled business models. (While both stories represent the personal experiences of the authors, some actors have been disguised to protect both the innocent and the guilty parties.)

## *Telco Tedium*

Taylor had been working hard at home all day analyzing large data sets and becoming increasingly frustrated with the glacial upload and download speeds of the household's telco provider. During the process, Taylor had seen an online ad from the telco provider for a new "quad play"—a package of four services at an attractive price that included superfast internet speeds. Seeking a solution to the day's frustrations, Taylor phoned the enterprise and got right through to a charming salesperson, Sasha. Sasha was professional and informed—really listening to Taylor's needs and proposing a customized quad play that would include superfast internet speeds, cable TV, house landline, and two of the newest-model cell phones. The call took about an hour, and the deal was done for a monthly fee and a new two-year contract.

Then the problems started. When Taylor and a family member visited the telco's retail store to pick out their new phones, the mobile-phone sales division knew neither who Taylor was nor what quad-play deal Taylor had purchased. Despite these initial problems, Taylor left with one working cell phone and a promise that the second phone would start working any minute. One week and four phone calls to the salesperson later, the second phone at last was up and running.

Meanwhile, the promised internet speed did not materialize. It turned out that Taylor's modem—which the telco had supplied the year before for a monthly rental fee—could not actually support the quad play's superfast internet abilities. Several phone calls later (during which Taylor provided identity information at least five times), the telco still hadn't resolved the modem problem. When the company finally did deliver the upgraded modem several weeks later, Taylor—normally technology astute—was flummoxed by the instructions. It took two more phone calls to the telco tech support before the household started enjoying a speedy internet. Over these many weeks, myriad additional problems emerged with the quad play, including a long delay getting the landline working (the connection was causing false alarms to the home-security service) and trouble with the pay-TV service— by which time Taylor had long since regretted having called the telco in the first place.

Several weeks later, Taylor attended a conference and, during a coffee break, recounted a short version of the telco story. An employee of that telco was within earshot and joined the conversation. He explained that although quad play was a brilliant marketing campaign that included well-trained call-center operators (like Sasha) and had already attracted the telco's best customers, that's where its brilliance ended. The trouble was that four separate business units provided each of the quad-play services, and since each unit acted as a silo, the units often had conflicting information about the customer. Worse still, when each business unit periodically upgraded the technical requirements to deliver on the quad play, that new information seldom made it into the training sessions for call-center operators.

The result? Sales at the telco skyrocketed—but frustration and net promoter scores (NPSs) plummeted, indicating that customers (particularly the telco's best customers) were less willing than ever before to recommend the telco to other potential customers. The enterprise had effectively snatched defeat from the jaws of victory.

## *Payment Perfection*

In contrast, Taylor had a much better experience getting prompt payment for some contract work done for a large consulting firm—at least, it was prompt once Taylor opted to use a digitized payment service. Up to that point, more than a month had passed since Taylor submitted an invoice, with still no payment in sight. Taylor did hear from the firm during that time: the accounting department requested that Taylor submit some forms to register as a vendor, a process that would take several more weeks to complete. And it cautioned that at least another four weeks would pass before the payment arrived.

Taylor might have despaired at this news had the accounting person not also mentioned a quicker, more efficient possibility: receive the firm's payment via PayPal. To do this, PayPal first needed to establish Taylor's one-person "company" as a PayPal customer. Taylor thought this step might take some effort, but a mere fifteen minutes after going to PayPal's website and following some simple instructions, Taylor had established the company as a vendor. Also within that time, the company had been verified as a legitimate enterprise and Taylor had submitted the invoice to the consulting firm. Six hours later, the invoice was paid in full with the consulting firm's credit card, via PayPal.

Perhaps this is an unfair comparison—contrasting a large telco with PayPal, a company often thought of as a startup. PayPal's revenues, however, are now approaching $10 billion globally, so it's not a startup anymore. But PayPal was born digital and, more to the point, fosters an internal digital culture.

What is stopping the telco from behaving like PayPal? The telco has access to the same people in the marketplace, the same technology, the same advisers, the same books and blogs on digital transformation, the same vendors, and so forth. But to succeed in the digital era, companies like the telco must focus on building their digital culture—that inimitable digital confidence, those shared values, beliefs, practices, and assumptions that guide behaviors in digitally enabled businesses.

In the remainder of this chapter, we'll return to the telco and Pay-Pal, as well as other companies, to illustrate how enterprises can build digital cultures and thereby reinvent themselves—specifically, by acquiring eight key capabilities. Before reading further, however, take a moment to revisit both parts of chapter 2's self-assessment, in which you identified where your enterprise stands today in the DBM framework. This is your starting point, and depending where you want to go, you can pick which of the eight capabilities are the most important to work on.

## Eight Capabilities for Reinvention

To illustrate what it takes to create a digital culture that delivers on top financial performance, we return to the DBM framework. Wherever your starting point is on the framework, the average financial performance of firms improves as those firms move up and to the right on the DBM framework. For example, on average in our studies, the enterprises that had high net margins were further up and to the right than were competitors—in other words, they knew more about their end customers and were more connected to digital ecosystems.[3]

Most large enterprises will choose to transform by moving first up and then to the right—becoming an ecosystem driver via the omnichannel model. They will provide the best service possible to their current customers today, selling their own products and services, through whatever channels the customer wants to use. (Fewer enterprises will move first to the right and then up, that is, from supplier to modular producer to ecosystem driver.) This move is more difficult because the transition from value chain to ecosystem requires a significant change in culture and some new technical capabilities.

To foster the transition up and to the right, then, we advise leaders of large enterprises to start investing in options today that will enable that reinvention. In the process, they will create a digital culture and learn what it takes to succeed in the digital economy while also improving performance. We've found that such reinvention hinges on the enterprise's acquiring eight key capabilities. Four of these capabilities move enterprises up on the DBM framework and improve their knowledge of the end customer and their ability to act on this knowledge. Four capabilities move enterprises to the right to shift it from a value chain to an ecosystem business design:

*Capabilities for moving up on the DBM framework:*

1. Gathering and using great information about customers' life events (e.g., their goals)

2. Amplifying the customer voice inside the enterprise (making the customer central to everything the enterprise does)

3. Creating a culture of evidence-based decision making (using customer, operational, market, and social data)

4. Providing an integrated, multiproduct, multichannel customer experience

### Capabilities for moving right on the DBM framework:

5. Being distinctive and the first place your best customers go when a need arises

6. Identifying and developing great partnerships and acquisitions

7. Service-enabling what makes you great—with exposed APIs

8. Developing efficiency, security, and compliance as competencies

Before we examine these two sets of capabilities in detail, consider Aetna's journey through all eight capabilities. The transformation required both top-down leadership by senior executives and bottom-up leadership by various departments (figure 5-1). As described earlier, Aetna is a $63.1 billion managed-health-care enterprise serving both individuals and employers, with a stated vision to "build a healthier world." The enterprise therefore is increasingly focusing on a multiproduct and multiservice customer experience that integrates the company's own products with third parties such as wellness services, health coaches, and other related services like credit cards. To help increase customer engagement—an area the enterprise needed to improve on—Aetna launched the very successful iTriage smartphone app to use when an accident or sickness happens.

Over fifteen years, Aetna's digital strategy moved the enterprise up and to the right on the DBM framework. Aetna went

FIGURE 5-1

## Aetna: Becoming an ecosystem driver

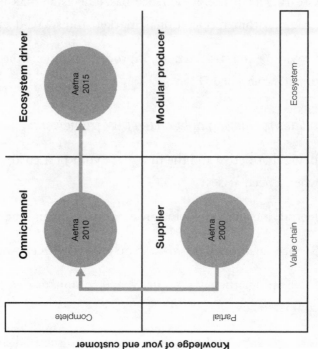

**Moving up**

- Shop, Buy, and Enroll Marketplace: an Amazon-like shopping experience
- Focus on attitudinal segments: basic, mainstream, best of everything
- 360-degree data view of the member
- NPS, Twitter, social-sentiment analysis
- Using analytics on data from multiple sources to optimize customer value
- A portfolio of products, services, and health and fitness apps

**Moving to the right**

- Be an attractive destination for health and wellness needs
- Acquisitions, including iTriage
- Partner with health insurance exchanges, providers, complementors, etc.
- Internal and affiliate APIs (e.g., member and plan profile) include additional health content, data, and services
- Expert on health-care compliance

*Source:* Interviews with Aetna executives, public sources, and Aetna.com. © 2017 MIT Sloan Center for Information Systems Research. Used with permission.

from being a supplier of health insurance (2000), to an omnichannel business that allowed customers to interact with Aetna easily on multiple channels (2010), to an ecosystem driver with digital capabilities to broker connections between the enterprise, its customers, and its partners.

For example, to better understand customers and amplify their voices inside the company (moving up on the framework), Aetna's IT organization led an effort to integrate multiple systems across the enterprise to provide a 360-degree data view of every member. To be more evidence-based, Aetna is using integration engines, business-rules engines, and data science insights to improve customer engagement and health-plan utilization. To increase the customers' voices inside the enterprise, Aetna uses NPSs, engages with customers on Twitter and other social media, and uses data analytics to track social-sentiments.

To move right, toward becoming an effective ecosystem driver, Aetna chose to become a destination for health and wellness needs—not health insurance—a radically different market position. To make the shift, Aetna had to develop a clear vision to become a new destination for customers, integrate a series of acquisitions and partnerships, and open up its business capabilities so that others could connect. For example, the IT group led a program to API-enable many of Aetna's key business capabilities so that internal colleagues and external affiliates could use them for innovation and to provide services. Aetna built a layered approach to support various systems of engagement; these systems include mobile, wearable platforms, and web apps. Security, management, scalability, and maintainability were significant architectural drivers for Aetna. The goal of enabling API integration was to bring a delightful and intuitive experience to the customer, like the experience delivered by the API-enabled integration of Aetna's traditional plan offerings with customer wellness offerings.

Looking to the future, Aetna will most likely continue its journey to become the leading ecosystem driver in health and wellness by offering more and more services that are increasingly integrated from a broad range of partners. We anticipate that Aetna will use the data it collects to improve its services and to make new offers to customers. Finally, types of services like iTriage will probably proliferate in many companies, with one or two companies becoming dominant in each domain.

Next, we'll examine the eight organizational capabilities in more detail and broken down into two sets: one set for moving up, and one for moving right on the DBM framework.

## Moving Up: Understanding End Customers Better and Acting on That Information

Moving up on the DBM framework is all about increasing the knowledge of your end customers and securing the four organizational capabilities to act on that insight. Equally important is the learning that accompanies each iteration of a capability.

1. **Gathering and using great information about customers' life events.** This capability is about using digital tools to obtain information about customers' goals and life events and then to act on them. Many enterprises, like the telco in our story recounted earlier, have customer data stored in separate departments, systems, and geographic locations, but they frequently can't deliver that data to a customer or an employee on his or her mobile device, during a phone call, or at a physical outlet at the moment

of truth—when the customer decides to engage. In contrast, what PayPal does very well is recognizing who you are. Today, Taylor in our story regularly uses PayPal both to get paid as a business owner and to make payments as a customer of other companies.

Many firms have a tough time gathering great information about customers without an effective organizing framework. There is so much data available, and without the guidance of a framework, it's very hard to know which data to focus on and what questions to ask. USAA's life-events model is a brilliant solution to this challenge. Identifying the customers' main life events, like buying a car, having a child, moving, and getting married provides a framework to focus the data-collection needs. Then for each life event, USSA identifies the set of connected products a customer needs to address that life event. This approach works equally well for B2B businesses, whose life events could include the enterprise's entrance into a new country, the launch of a new product, a merger, or a new CEO.

Of course, there are other ways to help organize the data, including customer journeys and more traditional customer segmentations. But for us, the life-events framework is very attractive because it forces the enterprise to reorganize its products and services to meet the life-event needs of the customers—rather than just pushing product. Take any large technology company— HP, IBM, Microsoft, Salesforce, Huawei, or SAP. One of the biggest challenges they face is to understand the life-event needs of a B2B customer and then quickly develop a unique solution for that customer by pulling together the different products and services provided by their different business units. The challenge is to make that customized solution truly fit the customer's needs while still reusing—and plugging and playing—the existing capabilities of the technology company. All too often, success relies on major heroics of a few people—typically the salespeople—using their internal connections to meet a customer's needs despite organizational friction. This internal friction often reduces the customer's satisfaction and can reduce the profitability of the engagement. Or worse, like the telco quad-play example, the customer gets vanilla services that aren't integrated or customized and he or she winds up feeling tossed from one internal service unit to another.

**2. Amplifying the customer voice inside the enterprise.** The amplification goes beyond simply using NPS or other measures of customer experience and satisfaction. It means really putting the customer at the center of the enterprise and using digitization to make customers' presence felt in every internal meeting and as part of every decision.

When a customer-centric enterprise looks at a metric like NPS, therefore, the enterprise will also add more contextual information, like customers' unvarnished sentiments via social media or focus groups, and will use big-data techniques and test-and-learn methodologies. Whatever techniques you use, the goal is to amplify the customer's voice inside your enterprise in every meeting room, in every decision, in every product design, every day, all the time. Only by making the customer's voice come to life in those critical moments inside the enterprise can you see real breakthroughs in understanding the customer (and moving up on the DBM framework).

For example, once Taylor began regularly using PayPal, Taylor started receiving certain communications—e.g., emails, offers for other services like point-of-sale terminals—that made it clear the company was checking on how well things were going and making adjustments accordingly. That is amplification.

Sadly, instead of true customer engagement, we often see heartfelt, isolated attempts to do big-data analysis or social-sentiment analysis with lovely charts, but the information acquired doesn't affect the decision making of the enterprise. Whatever technique you use, the question is how well it amplifies the customer's voice inside the enterprise. The techniques run the gamut from low-tech, high-touch to highly automated and are relevant to B2B and B2C. For example, LexisNexis—a B2B information provider—was a pioneer in converting customer understanding to action, investing heavily in strengthening its customer experience in 2010. In addition to the teams of anthropologists and sociologists described earlier, LexisNexis also works hard to give its customers a stronger voice. It carefully tracks customer satisfaction and is a sophisticated user of NPS. Surveys are sent to thousands of customers annually in many countries across all product and customer segments. The surveys are administered weekly with no one customer receiving more than two per year. LexisNexis calculates its NPS as a twelve-month rolling average. The key question—"How likely are you to recommend LexisNexis to a colleague?"—is rated on a 0–10 scale. Detractors, scoring 0–6, are unhappy customers. They get a red flag and are contacted by LexisNexis within twenty-four to forty-eight hours. Passive responders, scoring 7–8, are satisfied but open to competitors' offerings. Promoters, scoring 9–10, are enthusiastic customers and get a green flag. These customers are tapped to give testimonials and references.

NPS is reviewed at least weekly by senior management and is incorporated into individual performance reviews. Also, Lexis-Nexis uses an award-winning automated tracker at key customer touchpoints to highlight problems to be addressed before they affect the customer's overall relationship with LexisNexis.[4]

**3. Creating a culture of evidence-based decision making.** Many managers have historically relied on gut instinct and management experience to make crucial decisions about customer needs. However, in the era of big data, real-time dashboards, social-sentiment analysis, and many other sources of hard evidence, enterprises need to foster an evidence-based culture that requires many organizational changes. PayPal, for example, collects data from transactions and aggregates the data into measures of performance. Then, in light of those measures, the company creates actions to be directed at particular customers.

Another example is CIBC, a Tier 1 Canadian bank with global operations. CIBC is an omnichannel business, with numerous products sold across many channels in an integrated value chain. Because CIBC deals with its customers directly, the bank is the custodian of the customer relationship. The bank can aggregate customer data, perform customer analytics, and create innovative new products and services to better serve its customers. Most organizations segment their spending portfolio across their business units, which are often focused on their own segment of clients, locations, products, and regulatory environments. Key decisions that drive spending within each of these business units are based on information available to the units within their individual silos and are based on their local priorities. To successfully transform an organization, therefore, decisions made by business units need to come into alignment with predefined enterprise-wide strategies.

For CIBC, moving toward enterprise-coordinated decision making meant embarking on a bank-wide transformation that spanned its workforce, its suppliers, customer demand, bank processes, data, and digitization. These moves positioned the bank for competing within a digital ecosystem. CIBC created an evidence-based culture by providing the critical data to all key decision makers in a simple and consistent way. The bank relied on enterprise-architecture techniques, the organizing logic for key business processes and IT capabilities reflecting the integration and standardization requirements of the firm's operating model, to move the bank onto various shared-enterprise platforms. The platforms included data, customer information, product information, CRM, business-process orchestration, APIs, enterprise integration, user experience, cloud services, and digital identity of clients. That way, all the bank's different line-of-business efforts were building on the same foundations. This architecture reduced complexity, cost, and competing technologies, thereby facilitating digital development, improving agility, and accelerating time to market.[5]

**4. Providing an integrated, multiproduct, multichannel customer experience.** To make actual customer needs and goals central to the business model, enterprises need to stop pushing product and instead meet the customer's needs in the context of their life events. This change requires enterprises to develop integrated products across multiple channels simultaneously.

Integration is a hard transition for most enterprises. To understand the challenges just look at your local supermarket. Most supermarkets have added an online channel, but it's often poorly integrated into the physical channel. If physically based retailers are going to compete with online retailers like Amazon with its Amazon Fresh offering and its Whole Foods Market acquisition, they need to take advantage of their physical locations and seamlessly integrate—making their physical locations an asset rather than a liability. That integration requires more than adding the digital channel as an afterthought. Instead, the entire customer experience needs to be redesigned.

Amazon's Go—the name of the company's new physical stores—is a glimpse into what the redesigned store might look like. Using several technologies like computer vision, machine learning, and artificial intelligence, every item the shoppers select is tracked on their phone and as the shoppers exit, their bill is charged to their Amazon account.[6]

PayPal offers another good example of integration. On the DBM framework, PayPal operates as a modular producer for making payments that seamlessly integrate with any seller the PayPal customer picks. PayPal is also increasingly operating as an ecosystem driver by providing customers with a broader set of services to meet a targeted need—say, starting a small business. Small-business customers can use PayPal for payments, credit-card acceptance, point-of-sale processing, invoicing, borrowing funds for working capital, and more. The creation of such a multiproduct, multichannel customer experience is much easier for PayPal because it was born digital and isn't an omnichannel.

## Moving to the Right: From Value Chains to Ecosystem Business Design

Moving to the right is more challenging for most enterprises because it's about recognizing that your business is part of a bigger ecosystem that serves a broader set of customers. Moving to the right on the DBM framework means that an enterprise becomes either an ecosystem driver and the first choice for a subset of your customers or a modular producer working with other ecosystem drivers or both. In any of those cases, connectivity becomes a major issue, and the following four key capabilities become all-important to making the move to the right.

**5. Being distinctive—and the first place your best customers go to when a need arises.** When you think online payment, what enterprise do you think of first? For many people particularly in the United States, the answer is PayPal. This enterprise holds a distinctive space in the digital market and has found ways to make customers consider PayPal their go-to solution when it comes to payments. The company began as a modular producer, providing payment services to both ecosystem drivers and omnichannel businesses, with two distinct customers—merchants and end customers.

When it comes to distinctiveness in the retail space, Amazon is the first choice for many customers. Moreover, Aetna would like to be your first choice for health-care needs. Fidelity aims to be your first choice for wealth management, LexisNexis your first choice in legal services, and GE your first choice for the industrial internet. In the workshops we've done for large enterprises on digital transformation, what makes the enterprise distinctive is often the hardest for senior executive teams to answer. It really gets to the core of how you will differentiate your enterprise in a digital economy. Here is a list of some large enterprises and how we would describe the way they'll become the first choice—the go-to destination—in their spaces:

- **Aetna:** building a healthier world

- **GE:** building the industrial internet

- **LEGO:** inspiring and developing the builders of tomorrow

- **7-Eleven Japan:** solving your daily needs

- **WeChat:** providing for your daily life

- **BMW:** providing tailored mobility

- **Uber:** being your digital logistics mesh over a city

- **Amazon:** becoming your destination for . . . almost everything

This discussion brings us back to the question that began this chapter, in a sense, the question underlying this book and the whole topic of succeeding in the digital era: What makes your enterprise distinctive, and how will it become your customers' first choice in that distinctive space?

In workshops with individual large enterprises, we ask senior executives to break into small groups and answer that question. Everyone is surprised by the variation in answers across groups—an excellent reflection of how difficult it can be to create a compelling vision and then provide integrated customer experience across a large enterprise. Reaching agreement on the answer to this question is a terrific starting point for most enterprises' digital transformation.

**6. Identifying and developing great partnerships and acquisitions.** Ecosystem drivers have to find ways to partner with providers of complementary products and services and then integrate those offerings, such as payments, alerts, and delivery, into a seamless experience. The motivation for these partnerships is to better meet your customer's life-event needs.

To meet these needs, ecosystem drivers can include partnerships with both complementors and competitors. For example, USAA AutoCircle partners with car dealers to provide USAA customers a great deal on car purchases, complementing USAA's services. Sometimes, meeting the customer's needs also means partnering with competitors, such as how customers of Fidelity can purchase Vanguard funds at Fidelity.com. Fidelity still keeps the primary relationship with the customer while offering a wide choice of mutual funds by including competitors like Vanguard and others.

Modular producers live and die by their ability to partner with ecosystem drivers. For example, PayPal and the myriad of other payment service providers have to be easy to use, must operate in many compliance environments, and must allow seamless plug-and-play in other enterprises' systems. PayPal has been exceptionally good at these partnerships, operating in more than a hundred countries. Sometimes, ecosystem drivers make the partnership permanent. Acquisitions can be a wonderful way to fast-track a great strategy, and the digital era raises the stakes for picking and integrating acquisitions. For example, Aetna acquired iTriage, saving years of development time, and then worked hard to link Aetna's digitized products and services to the app to deliver a world-class service directly at the point of need.

**7. Service-enabling what makes you great (with exposed APIs).** Digital is a lot about connecting different products and silos in the enterprise to improve the customer experience. It's also about making the enterprise part of a digital ecosystem to provide the best options for the customer at all times. You need to take what capabilities make you great as an enterprise—your crown jewels, those core business capabilities like producing a product, processing an insurance claim or loan application, writing a proposal, providing advice, booking an airplane seat—and turn them into digitized services. Then make those digitized services easily and securely available throughout your business—and to your partners and customers.

How do you make these digitized services? First, you review and standardize your business rules. Second, you digitize the business capabilities according to those business rules and create interfaces to access them. Many enterprises provide the interfaces with their core capabilities to both insiders and outsiders to help drive faster innovation.

For example, one problem with the telco in our earlier story was that it had more than twenty ways to onboard a new customer and more than thirty-five ways to sell an existing customer a new product. This complex landscape of business processes, systems, and data helped thwart the seamless delivery of the quad-play promise. Only through the heroics of the telco's customer agents on the phone and in the store was the customer able to get through this maze. By contrast, PayPal has developed only a few ways to do these onboarding processes, and it created a platform and APIs that can be used both inside the company for new offerings and externally by merchants who use the PayPal payment service.

The most common approach to service enablement is deploying APIs. We saw a strong difference across top- and bottom-performing companies in terms of their net margins and the percentages of accessible APIs. Among top-quartile performers on margin, 51 percent of key enterprise capabilities were available internally, and 44 percent were available externally. For bottom-quartile performers, only 27 percent were available internally, and 23 percent externally.[7]

Consider examining how your own enterprise compares with those percentages. Whose job is it to make such connectivity happen?

**8. Developing efficiency, security, and compliance as competencies.** This is the eighth and final item in the list of capabilities that successful enterprises undertake when they reinvent themselves for the digital age. As leaders of top performers digitize their operations, they also recognize the potential efficiencies, responsibilities, and threats. Let's start with the responsibilities and threats. Enterprises that can more effectively deal with data privacy, cyber threats, potential service disruptions, and the need for increasing levels of compliance with governments and other regulators worldwide will make compliance a competence, not a chore. For example, any company operating as an ecosystem driver or a modular producer can offer many of these compliance services to its customers. More and more companies, such as PayPal, BNY Mellon, and Fidelity, offer services to their customers to help them understand and comply with US government regulations.

We've observed two very different enterprise attitudes toward dealing with compliance. The first is what we call the woe-is-me approach. It goes like this: Our industry and, particularly, our enterprise are just getting hammered with increasing compliance requirements from many agencies. Some of these demands are unreasonable, and all of them are a pain. Meeting these requirements is taking an increasing amount of our time and budget and creates little bottom-line value.

The second attitude, which we are increasingly seeing among top performers, falls along these lines: Compliance is a fact of life, and the increasing compliance requirements are a part of our right to do business. Perhaps we, and our competitors, have brought some of this increased compliance on ourselves. So we are going to become great at compliance and be better at it than our competitors are. We will also use compliance to help clean up how we manage our business. In short, we will make compliance a competence.

This second attitude reflects a certain necessary ambidexterity that we've seen from enterprises that successfully reinvent themselves for the digital age. With one hand, they need to innovate, excite customers, and create new value. With the other hand, they need to become more efficient and decrease costs by, say, 5 percent every year. The enterprises mastering ambidextrousness will have a significant advantage in the digital economy. The challenge is that the culture, organizational structure, and mindset to do both at the same time is very difficult and is typically not the way enterprises work today. Innovation and efficiency have historically had different DNAs, and enterprises usually go through cycles where they focus on each for a time and then switch, often driven by economic conditions. In the digital economy, the left and the right hands will need to work together, and enterprises will have to learn to excel at innovation and cost reduction at the same time.

## How Good Is Your Enterprise at the Eight Key Capabilities?

As you read through the previous section, you were most likely thinking about your own enterprise and how good you are at each of the eight key capabilities. Use the chapter 5 self-assessment to evaluate your own enterprise. If you gave each question the top score of 6 and follow the scoring guide, you would get a total score of 96. Leaders in the digital economy typically have scores of 70 or higher (only 8 percent of companies). How do you compare? And which are your top two and bottom two scores? Your top score tells you what you can use to make improvements in other areas: a top evidence-based decision-making score will help you treat security and compliance as a capability that you will measure and continuously improve over time. The bottom scores

CHAPTER 5

## Self-assessment

**How effective is your enterprise at the following (1 = Not effective, 6 = Very effective)?**

- Gathering and using great information about customer life events

- Amplifying the customer voice inside the enterprise

- Creating a culture of evidence-based decision making

- Providing an integrated, multiproduct, multichannel customer experience

- Being distinctive and the first place your best customers go when a need arises

- Identifying and developing great partnerships and acquisitions

- Service-enabling core business transactions (with exposed APIs)

- Developing efficiency, security, and compliance as competencies

*Add up your scores and double the total (out of 96) =*

*Source:* © 2017 MIT Sloan Center for Information Systems Research. Used with permission.

will tell you where you have to focus your attention today. Typically, the bottom score is the weak link in the chain—and sadly, the chain often breaks.

In a recent workshop we conducted for a financial services enterprise, twenty-two of the senior management team members assessed their company. Their top scores were for treating efficiency, compliance, and security as competencies. Their lowest scores were for service-enabling their core business transactions, gathering good information on life events, and amplifying the customer voice inside the enterprise. In an aha moment, the group saw the large variation in the executives' scores within each question. The leaders then discussed why the scores varied so much. The conversation greatly helped the executives build a shared understanding of the issues, including why digital excellence was patchy across the enterprise. Then we broke into teams. Each team picked one of the eight items to work on and proposed some innovative ways to achieve breakthroughs.

———————

By now, you should have a good sense of where your enterprise is on the DBM framework and where you'd like to go. You should also grasp how good your enterprise is at the eight key capabilities required to move up and to the right on that framework.

## How BBVA Set the Vision for Reinvention and Changed the Culture

Finally, we wanted to address two broader issues we are often asked about in workshops when we speak of reinvention: how to set the vision for change, and how to carry out the organizational surgery needed to enact that change. BBVA offers a good example on how to do both.

As noted earlier, Francisco González, group executive chairman of BBVA, declared in 2015, "We are building the best digital bank of the 21st century."[8] BBVA worked hard at removing the IT spaghetti that had built up over time because of its many systems and replacing it with efficient, scalable global platforms. These platforms combine optimized business processes, efficient technology, and easily accessible data at a relatively low cost—while meeting the company's regulatory needs.[9]

The vision and cultural changes were summarized into six strategic priorities to help achieve the chairman's declaration: create a new standard in customer experience; drive digital sales; develop new business models; optimize capital allocation; obtain an unrivaled efficiency; and, finally, develop, inspire, and retain a first-class workforce.

But it was going to be challenging to achieve the strategic goals without changing the organizational structure and culture. To achieve these strategic goals, BBVA announced in May 2015 some major organizational changes to move a step closer to the vision of a digital bank. The company showed its commitment to digital by appointing Carlos Torres Vila—former head of digital banking—as CEO.

Here are some key organizational features and changes of the BBVA transformation:

- *Strategic focus located at the top:* Strategy control remains with Group Executive Chairman Francisco González. The elements remaining under his control include legal and compliance issues, strategy, mergers and acquisitions, global economics and public affairs, communications, accounting and supervisors, and internal audit functions. González believes that these are the executive chairman's issues. And by keeping these issues under González's management, CEO Torres Vila is freed up to transform and manage the bank day-to-day.

- *New organizational structure:* The new structure separates execution and performance from new core competencies. Groups where leaders are focused on serving customers and selling—the country networks and the corporate and investment banking groups—sit under execution and performance. Under the new core competency of engineering, the bank has combined operations, IT, and some products to provide banking services enterprise-wide and across all the country networks.

- *Combining the best existing talent with new people:* As part of this transformation, the bank looked carefully at the senior executive teams and asked some of the leaders to continue playing major roles in the bank. In addition, the bank looked outside for leaders, particularly in the new core competency areas, and several came from outside the banking industry.

- *New approaches to work:* Along with the new organizational structure, BBVA has adopted some fresh approaches to getting work done. For example, it has embraced agile methods at scale. Hundreds of multidisciplinary, dedicated scrum teams work together to develop new features in two-week sprints with quarterly planning to ensure systematic, accountable, and transparent project management.

- *Overhauled talent and culture division:* The overhaul had two goals—attract and retain the best and most needed talent and create a more agile and enterprising corporate culture. The bank needed to embrace new cultural values (like "fail fast, fail often," a test-and-learn mentality, and empowerment through accountability) while working to eliminate hierarchical structures.

The early results are very encouraging, with BBVA achieving number one or number two in customer experience in its top countries.[10] Digital sales are about 25 percent of total sales. And in July 2017 a Forrester Research report cited BBVA's Spanish business as having the world's best mobile banking app.[11] Throughout its reinvention, BBVA has learned several important lessons, including the following:

- Digital transformation requires a strong vision, with leadership often making hard decisions.

- The importance of being a purpose-driven company.

- The importance of speeding up execution.

- The importance of gaining customer trust.

- Digital transformation requires a single team with a single plan. For example, the formerly separate groups of IT, business units, and user experience—both local and global—now work together in agile scrum teams.

- Being digital also means the emergence of new roles (designers, software developers, data scientists, etc.) that need the best talent from both inside and outside the enterprise.

- The enterprise leaders have to find the right balance between a pragmatic and a visionary approach. The bank has to continue to operate, make money, and serve customers well, while it undergoes transformation, and that requires many difficult trade-offs along the way.

- Finally, the leaders must get the entire organization, including every person in the branch network, onboard. Every employee has to play a role in the new digitally transformed enterprise. Most important, they need to feel like part of the team and believe that their contributions matter.

---

In this chapter, you've discussed ways to reinvent your enterprise for the digital age. On completing this chapter, you should understand many aspects of your enterprise's reinvention:

- Where your enterprise is on the DBM framework today (see the chapter 2 assessment)

- Where you want to go on the DBM framework (your judgment call, with assistance from examples in chapters 2, 3, and 4)

- How effective your enterprise is today on the eight key capabilities (self-assessment in this chapter)

- Which of these eight capabilities you need to work on (your lowest scores in this chapter's self-assessment)

- Some ideas from the company examples in this chapter on how to improve your enterprise's capabilities with the lowest scores

Now the question becomes, *Where do you need to start to reinvent the enterprise?* It's up to you now. In the final chapter, we will focus on the leadership required to make the changes needed.

**CHAPTER 6**

# Do You Have the Leadership to Make Your Transformation Happen?

People sometimes ask us what the best part of our jobs at MIT is. The answer is easy. It's when we engage with a small group of senior leaders as they make the elephant that is their large enterprise nimble and elegant on the dance floor. It's the thrill of watching companies like Aetna transforming health care, BBVA changing financial services, Schneider Electric rethinking energy services, Dunkin' Donuts and 7-Eleven Japan reinventing customer engagement in franchise-based food networks—or the ongoing reimagining of the many other enterprises described in this book.[1]

To be sure, the visionary and persistent leaders of these enterprises orchestrate the transformation that enables improved performance, connectivity, customer engagement, and employee experience. But those transformations are only possible because most employees, most customers, and most partners of the enterprise actually want to make things better every day. Again and again, most people come to work hoping they can perform well and help their enterprise be great.

Too often, however, organizational speed bumps make change difficult.[2] Think of the onerous governance processes, complex interlocking committees, outdated work practices, poor tools, stultifying command-and-control cultures, leaders who don't want to change the status quo, and other change-resistant cultures. Some of these speed bumps were built for good reasons in the past—but need revisiting now. Others just happened and need fixing.

As we begin this chapter, you will have thought through where you currently sit on the DBM framework and where you would like to be. Some companies will move from supplier to omnichannel and eventually to ecosystem drivers. Others will move from having nascent omnichannel capabilities to becoming a great omnichannel enterprise. Others will move from supplier to modular producer but just for part of the business. And so on. To succeed in whatever model on the DBM framework you are targeting, your enterprise must undergo a transformation. You must change the way you do things, perhaps radically, and recognize that because you won't get it right the first time, you'll need to iterate and course-correct.

This chapter is all about how to successfully implement that transformation. In it, we look at one important decision that top leaders must make in creating the next-generation enterprise: they must identify and support the people in the organization who will help lead the change. Finding and supporting leaders is undoubtedly one of the hardest parts of a business-model change. But giving your people challenges with the right resources and support and watching them develop and achieve those goals is potentially the most satisfying job a leader can have.

A commitment to transformation requires identifying leaders from all parts of the organization—from the top down and the bottom up. No matter which of the four ways your enterprise will make money as a next-generation enterprise—as a supplier, an omnichannel, a module producer, or an ecosystem driver— you will have to transform your enterprise to be a top performer, and that will take significant commitment from everyone in the enterprise.

In this chapter, we'll explore the roles of four important groups in any major transformation: the board, the CEO and executive committee, the CIO, and the workforce (including middle management and newer hires). We illustrate the leadership challenges, with insights from Deloitte, ING, Microsoft, and DBS Bank. We also offer an assessment for you to evaluate your people and culture, and we end with recommendations for how to begin leading the change to the next-generation enterprise.

But first, let's begin with some lessons learned from one company's successful transformation—and how the board, the CEO and executive committee, the CIO, and the workforce helped move the changes forward.

## Transformation: How One Financial Services Company Made the Hard Choices

One of the most successful transformations we've witnessed was a financial services enterprise that evolved from a medium-performing bank, primarily a supplier with some omnichannel capabilities, to one of the world's top banks on most metrics. The change began with a visionary board that appointed a new CEO who was given aggressive performance targets. The board was a diverse group; it included several directors with strong experience in technology-driven businesses, some experienced bankers, a consultant or two, and some economists. The board recognized that to have a step change in performance, the bank would have to transform itself, and the board would have to support changing the business model, shifting personnel and making significant investments over a number of years. Understanding the bank's current business model, the board members educated themselves on the likely prospects for the bank as the industry became more competitive and digital. They consulted thought leaders and other noncompeting bankers and made updates on progress a part of the regular board agenda. The board also added a subcommittee on digital threats, including cybersecurity, acceptable data use, regulatory compliance, and system outages.

The CEO realized that to achieve the aggressive performance targets, the enterprise would need to substantially improve its omnichannel capabilities (moving up on the DBM framework) as well as acquire options by starting both ecosystem-driver and modular-producer businesses. At the same time, the bank had to reduce the cost to serve customers. Customer experience at the beginning of the transformation (which eventually stretched to eight years) was about average relative to competitors, so the CEO chose to start by building a new set of shared banking-service capabilities that would be efficient and modular. The customer experience could then be reinvented with the new capabilities, which included a common customer database, a core banking platform, and a multichannel customer-experience platform. The CEO evaluated the executive committee and appointed several new people, moving some of the current executives to different jobs and asking others to leave the bank altogether.

One of the biggest changes the CEO made was to shift the culture of the executive committee. The CEO had inherited a set of powerful leaders, each executive having almost total discretion on delivering the performance results for his or her individual business. But in an omnichannel model, this type of executive committee doesn't work as well: you don't get an integrated multiproduct, multichannel customer experience with siloed businesses or functions. Instead, the executive committee needs to act as a team because much of the transformation happens across business units and functions. With this difference in mind, the CEO changed not only the makeup of the executive committee, but also how it operated. Gone was the individual "star culture," which was replaced by a team that had joint accountability for transforming the bank.

Accordingly, the CEO held the executive committee jointly accountable for two metrics: (1) becoming number one in customer experience, measured externally, and (2) having the best cost-to-income ratio measured against peers. Instead of running their own individual businesses as star players might do, the executive committee members worked together to help the bank and each other succeed. Meetings of the executive committee changed. Previously, each star advocated for the changes desired for his or her own business and wasn't particularly engaged in what happened elsewhere in the bank. In the new executive committee, the CIO played a key leadership role and all members were interested in all the critical decisions made in the bank. This sense of joint accountability and joint rewards made them more willing to help each other and compromise for the good of the whole bank.

The CIO's role was expanded to include both IT and operations, and more recently, digital. The CIO also ran the core banking-transformation project that required significant consolidation of business processes and product rationalization. Among other duties, the CIO had to spend much more time helping the executive committee and peers make the difficult decisions about which products to cut and which processes to standardize.

Because of the new team culture, the executive committee could facilitate discussions about the parts of the business that had proven challenging under the previous model. For example, the committee could now readily discuss how to standardize key business processes, how to rationalize the product set, and how to clearly identify who was accountable for which customers. A big proportion of the financial incentives for each executive committee member depended on the whole committee's reaching its joint goals—another big change.

The changes made at the executive committee soon percolated throughout the entire organization. Reduced but, of course, not entirely gone were the individual political contests that had occurred across business units and the inter-unit struggles for resources. One noticeable change was a strong drive to industrialize the bank, a step that would reduce costs, increase customer responsiveness, and improve how quickly the bank could respond to changes in the market. The bank held many workshops and other education programs and used new tools to design those new business processes and find the best way to do things. Once the core banking platform was implemented, the executive committee nurtured a culture of innovation to get the most out of the big shared core banking investment. Everyone in the company was encouraged to innovate—to create new products and services on the platform. There was widespread recognition that the bank had built a shared set of assets that everybody owned, nurtured, and could utilize.

In summary, the three big changes the CEO and colleagues made to the enterprise can apply to other organizations aiming for a successful transformation:

- **Top-down first:** Make transformation choices from the top down, indicate the desired pace of change, and specify indicators of success with the active buy-in of the board. Then pick the key people to lead the change and create a team with shared goals and measures of success.

- **Communicate:** Communicate the transformation widely both internally and externally, and create expectations (supported by training, empowerment, and incentives) that the teams in the organization need to act differently to achieve the enterprise transformation goals. The result is often a remarkable number of bottom-up efforts that help transform the enterprise. In the bank we've just described, the outcomes included a bottom-up consolidation effort to reduce the number of credit-scoring processes from more than twenty down to two.

- **Drive and reinforce the cultural change:** Almost by definition, the culture that led the enterprise to the point where it needed to transform is not the culture required to complete the transformation. But culture is hard to change, and not all elements of an existing culture are bad. The idea is to pick the cultural elements that your enterprise will need and then demonstrate and reinforce those behaviors repeatedly. New people in key roles can help change the culture, but most people will get excited about making significant improvements to the enterprise and will change how they operate if they believe in the transformation. Social media—which we will return to later—has proven to be a powerful tool in flattening hierarchies, sharing successes, and reinforcing a questioning and ambidextrous culture.

Now that we've described what transformation looks like, let's examine each of the key roles everyone needs to play in the enterprise to make the needed changes.

## Key Roles in a Transformation

Who will work to create the transformation needed to succeed in the next-generation enterprise? Here we look at the four major groups: the CEO and executive committees, the board, the workforce, and the CIO.

### *CEO and the Executive Committees*

As the role of the CEO grows increasingly challenging, successful CEOs will become adept at identifying what they will focus on and what can be delegated to others. In virtually all the successful transformations we have studied, the CEO has played an important role, but has also involved and delegated many of the activities to a handful of carefully selected people who get it.

The main tasks of the CEO are to commit to a transformation and monitor progress; to drive and reinforce the cultural change required; and to sell, resell, and communicate the vision both internally and externally. And the most important—and perhaps the hardest task—the chief executive must pick the right team members, motivate them, give them the right incentives, and keep them on track. Finally, only the CEO can perform the organizational surgery when it's necessary, redoing the structure, budgets, decision rights, cultural norms, and incentives as well as shouldering other responsibilities to promote success, like engaging the board.

Any transformation will require organizational surgery of some type. We've learned that the executive committee will not perform organizational surgery on itself. There are too many vested interests and potential winners and losers among the members for self-inflicted surgery. Instead, the CEO, after consulting with the board and other advisers, will have to decide that organizational surgery is necessary and will pick the winners and losers on the executive committee. Given that the CEO often must act as the surgeon, the role and the support of the board becomes very important, as we will discuss in the next section. (For a snapshot on the important changes made by Schneider Electric's executive committee, see the sidebar "Schneider Electric Makes Changes from the Top.")

## The Board

One group with increasing importance in digital disruption and transformation is the enterprise's board of directors. Although, as we've just described, CEOs must lead this organizational transformation, they nevertheless will need increasing support and the occasional nudge from a well-informed and interested board. Beyond the board's normal fiduciary and oversight responsibilities, it plays a key role dealing with the challenges of digital disruption and transformation. One of the biggest decisions enterprises face is how they should reorganize to be effective in a digital era—the surgery.[3]

## Schneider Electric Makes Changes from the Top

Schneider Electric's Chairman and CEO, Jean-Pascal Tricoire, and his executive committee were the architects and leaders of the enterprise's change to digital. But of course, they couldn't do it alone, and they relied on many others they trusted along the way. Among the many ways Schneider Electric involved its board and all employees in the transformation, it organized several off-site strategy sessions on how digital would dramatically change the company's business.

Creating a digital culture in a large, complex global enterprise is probably the most challenging aspect of a transformation. All too often, we see multiple digital cultures in large enterprises that may create local value but don't achieve the promise of digital— connecting the silos to deliver a new, exciting customer-value proposition. Schneider Electric's leadership recognized this challenge and started with the cultural change from the top down. Historically, senior management had three types of periodic management reviews: the business, the people, and the strategy. It added a fourth review, the role of digital. The executive committee, which meets each year to prioritize investments, decided to place a big bet on digital services with centralized capabilities.

To help foster a digital culture, Schneider Electric established two new units: digital customer experience and digital services. The digital customer-experience organization is responsible for designing the digital customer journeys. The digital services organization looks after digital business transformation, which includes helping businesses transform and managing their digital operations.

Another key initiative was to develop "playbooks" for each business to support scaling its digital transformation. The playbooks capture best-practice experience from long-term employees to describe what should be managed locally versus globally. These tools also clarify the differences across the twelve go-to-market models (e.g., the software business is more centralized than the retail businesses, because of retail's local requirements). The playbooks spell out the main roles for each business. To help spread the digital culture across the enterprise, Schneider Electric created an internal academy modeled on massive open online courses. In this open academy, everyone in Schneider Electric can access the digital playbooks and build skills. And to provide a voice to all, a wiki, begun at Schneider Electric in 2015, allows people to contribute their thoughts on each business and each playbook, enabling everyone to learn from everyone else's experiences—effectively flattening the organization's hierarchy.

Schneider's senior executive team understood that to truly transform the company, the company culture had to become digitally savvy. And this transformation would have a beginning but no end as the company, its industry, and the economy would become increasingly connected.

Fortunately, boards themselves understand that supporting the CEO is one of their main jobs. In one study we conducted, board directors identified "challenging the status quo" as the second-most important activity (after "evaluating the CEO") that boards carry out among the legal, moral, and fiduciary responsibilities they have to stakeholders. What's more, many board members saw digital disruption as one of the biggest threats to the enterprise, estimating that 32 percent of their enterprises' revenues are threatened by such disruption over the next five years; if the enterprises did nothing, they would lose this revenue.

Yet despite that concern and their desire to support transformation, much of the governance focus on digital disruption at enterprises has been on cybersecurity, data privacy, compliance, and spending on IT. Only 39 percent of board members reported discussing the impact of digitization itself on the enterprise's business model.

The reason for this lack of focus? Our studies show that it might be lack of digital-savvy board members. While boards are warming to the task of advocating for and advising on enterprise digital transformations, their self-reported scores show that the boards have work to do to increase their own digital knowledge.

For example, board members rated their own digital knowledge at only 62 percent (i.e., they gave themselves a D-minus) and rated their fellow directors as only 64 percent effective in dealing with digital disruption. Such lack of digital aptitude has led 45 percent of boards to hire consultants to evaluate major digital projects, because they didn't feel comfortable making those evaluations themselves.[4] This situation raises the stakes for the quality of input that board members need from their enterprise executives. And the quality of input from those executives is currently mixed. When asked to assess the effectiveness of their officer-level executives in helping board members deal with digital disruption, CIOs were ranked as the most effective (82 percent effective), followed by CEOs (78 percent) and heads of marketing (70 percent). Heads of HR were deemed least helpful (62 percent).

All this matters immensely because the enterprise's board members must ultimately be convinced by any new vision for transformation. They must understand that the transformation is good for the enterprise's long-term health and that it's achievable. Then the board needs to provide the capital required for the transformation and must support the CEO when he or she makes the difficult and necessary organizational changes.

Clearly, then, to help their enterprises and CEOs navigate the digital economy, board members require new skills. The directors' longtime business experience will continue to be valuable but will be only part of what the directors need if they are to effectively perform their roles. Understanding which business models will be important to their enterprise's digital future—and helping to make the hard decisions about how and when to transform—will be critical.

Toward that end, we offer here three digitization activities that boards should perform: defense, oversight, and strategy (figure 6-1).

**Defense.** Focusing on defense issues helps prevent serious problems for the enterprise, including cyber risk, data privacy breaches, service interruptions, and compliance issues. Most boards deal with these issues through their audit or risk committees. Boards are becoming increasingly mature in these defensive areas and have built up sophisticated reporting and monitoring systems. Boards scored 71 percent for defensive activities—the highest effectiveness of the three roles.[5] We suggest that a risk subcommittee attend to defense issues and provide a brief report to the full

FIGURE 6-1

## Key board roles for digital

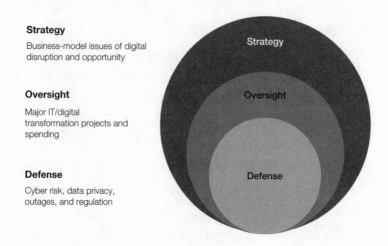

**Strategy**

Business-model issues of digital disruption and opportunity

**Oversight**

Major IT/digital transformation projects and spending

**Defense**

Cyber risk, data privacy, outages, and regulation

The sizes of the circles in the figure represent the scope of the roles. Boards have often focused on the narrower defense activities but need to broaden their scope to provide oversight and input to enterprise strategy.

board at each meeting; serious issues should be escalated to the whole board.

**Oversight.** The second role is oversight of the enterprise's major digitally enabled transformation projects. These projects include the implementation of large, mission-critical systems such as enterprise resource planning, patient records, and core banking. These systems are transformational investments that demand significant change-management efforts, monitoring, and oversight. For many enterprises, particularly banks, retailers, hospitals, media companies, and other enterprises that rely heavily on digital technologies, oversight also includes reviewing the spending levels on digitization across the enterprise and comparing goals and bottom-line impacts achieved. With the increasing impacts of digitization, enterprises are doing more oversight of digital investments across multiple business units. Boards scored 61 percent on effectiveness of oversight activities.

In our statistical analysis, we saw very little relationship between enterprises that were good at oversight at the board level and financial performance. Therefore, we suggest that oversight of major transformation projects be automated as much as possible into a dashboard that's available to board members anytime. The dashboard would highlight serious issues for discussion. We suggest that management's numerous, lengthy presentations on the progress of major projects be removed from general board meetings and that a subcommittee monitor the dashboard for serious issues.

**Strategy.** The third role for board members involves their contributing to and evaluating conversations about strategy and digital disruption. Among all the board activities evaluated, boards overall scored the lowest (53 percent) on effectiveness of digital strategy.

Even though boards are sometimes not particularly effective (yet) at contributing to discussions of digital strategy, the pressure from digitization is pushing them to have those conversations anyway. For example, a number of banks reported that boardroom conversations about digital strategy have focused not on other banks, as in the past, but on market entrants such as PayPal, Apple Pay, Square, Amazon, Google and retailers that are potentially nibbling away at their revenues. These new entrants threaten to relegate some banks to highly regulated, low-margin, transactional processors of payments. With the increasing importance of disruptive technologies and the potential of the IoT, most enterprise strategies will need to change. For example, the

head of strategy for Emerson, a $14.5 billion diversified manu-
facturer, said, "In the twenty-first century, we will differentiate
our enterprise and provide value to our customers and returns
to our shareholders through trading on information."[6] Emerson's board takes an active role in conversations about digital
strategy issues.

The most effective mechanism for working on strategy was
retreats, where external speakers and internal leaders presented
their ideas briefly, followed by extensive discussion and exercises.
Also very effective were internal and external case studies of success and failures and visits to both similar and different enterprises that were successful in digital transformation.

For improving the digital savvy of boards, two other mecha-
nisms were effective. First, peer ratings, through which the board
members assessed their peers on their contributions, were very
helpful and could be implemented in many ways. For instance,
the lead director (or chair) could meet with each of the other directors to collect peer-review information or could gather the information via surveys or a consultant. Overall ratings or other
feedback is shared with board members, increasing transparency
and, hopefully, the value added over time.

Second, several boards reported successful reverse-mentoring
programs in which the board members were paired up with
younger employees. The pairs met regularly, say, once a quarter,
and mentored each other. The board members reported excellent experiences, often learning things like how millennials use
mobile devices, what is really happening in the enterprise (at least
from the reverse mentor's perspective), and other trends they otherwise wouldn't hear about. Naturally, the younger mentors were
delighted with the opportunity not only to influence board members, but also to learn from them.

## *Workforce*

Transformation offers a wonderful opportunity to unlock what should be the most precious resource in your enterprise—your people—and empower them to make your enterprise even better. DBS Bank, Asia's largest banks, offers an exemplar.[7] In its recent transformation revamping its omnichannel model, the bank developed a series of initiatives that empowered its employees and gave the transformation legs.

Founded in 1968 in Singapore (where it is also headquartered), DBS has a major presence in five Asian countries as well as operations in the United States and Europe. It has had a spectacular record of growth and profitability, outperforming its industry and earning the name "world's best digital bank" at the July 2016 Euromoney awards.

To accomplish those feats, DBS began exploiting digital around 2010 to reinvent itself, with one primary focus: to unleash the creative potential of all its employees to help DBS innovate in its particularly competitive market and more recently to make banking joyful. For example, DBS hired a chief innovation officer to lead a new Innovation Office and Council that coordinated the various innovation efforts at the bank and standardized on a common methodology and language for innovation.

At the same time, DBS began several talent and culture initiatives, including innovation training workshops for staff and profiling and recruiting people with strong innovation potential. Examples of successful innovations were circulated throughout DBS as a way of boosting employees' confidence in putting forward innovation ideas. "Being innovative" and being "a catalyst for change" also became good criteria for promotions.

DBS also began crowdsourcing innovative ideas from its employees. For example, uGOiGO, a group-buying campaign focused on online term deposits, was started by DBS Hong Kong in 2013. The campaign targeted affluent customers using social media. More attractive, tiered interest rates for term deposits were triggered once the deposit amounts hit specific targets. The new product launch was a tremendous success.

Many more digital innovations followed including the launching of Digibank in India we described earlier, with paperless account opening in 90 seconds, attracting 1 million new customers in just one year.[8]

The result was more innovation, driving more revenue growth and cost savings, with more engaged and committed DBS employees and happier customers. To give all employees a simple but common goal, DBS senior management chose as a key performance indicator the number of customer-hours saved as they engaged with DBS. The combined efforts from several initiatives including, mapping customer journeys, automation, and data analytics, well surpassed the customer-hours target. So far, DBS's improvements have saved 250 million customer hours while also improving internal productivity, saving 1 million employee hours. This metric of customer-hours saved is carefully tracked and regularly reported within DBS and has proved a unifying goal.

To achieve these changes, DBS asks its senior leadership to be more facilitative and less directive—more innovative and less focused on control. For example, leaders conduct regular hackathons in which bankers team up with young coders for a week to embed digital thinking and skills through experiential learning. The result: as of November 2017, 14,800 of the approximately 22,000 DBS employees were actively engaged in sixteen different innovation programs.[9]

Piyush Gupta, CEO of the bank, explains the transformation as a move toward the bank of tomorrow, which will "look fundamentally different from banks today." For DBS, the transformation meant changing the bank's culture, Gupta says, "re-architecting our technology infrastructure and leveraging Big Data, biometrics, and artificial intelligence to make banking simple and seamless for customers."[10]

An important element to consider when looking at your workforce (and ways to empower it toward digitization) is the younger staff in the enterprise. Just as DBS holds hackathons between leaders and younger employees, so too can your business take advantage of the digital knowledge your youngest colleagues have to share. This is not to say that others in the workforce are not also digitally savvy; after all, digitizing your enterprise is not just a young person's game. The digital wave is hitting everyone, and we are all rising on it. But in most organizations, young people can be the most disenfranchised, the most disconnected, and the least heard. What they lack in experience they often make up for with enthusiasm for change and all things digital. There are many ways to value and involve the young people of your enterprise. One of the most promising involves the use of social media.

For example, in a very successful transformation effort, Deloitte Australia changed the cultural norms, using social media to give everyone a voice. Our MIT CISR colleagues Kristine Dery, Ina Sebastian, and Jeanne Ross explain Deloitte's strategy: "At a time when most organizations had banned the use of Facebook and other social media, Deloitte took a radical approach and made social media central to its strategic transformation."[11] By setting up an account with Yammer, the internal social media site for individual organizations, Deloitte made it easy for every layer of the hierarchy to begin, or engage with, the corporate conversation.

The senior leaders initiated and joined Yammer discussions daily, stimulating new ideas and listening to online discussions to glean insights into ways to improve workplace effectiveness. People connected in new ways as they focused their attention and skills around ideas rather than siloed services.

"Sourcing of ideas became much more transparent," the authors say, "and new champions emerged, many of whom had previously been invisible. Facebook, LinkedIn, and Twitter are integral to the new way of working at the enterprise, both internally and externally. All employees are expected to be fully engaged in social media and to be brand ambassadors in all their activity." Analysis at Deloitte provides evidence of a strong association between collaboration, connectivity, and performance.

## *Chief Information Officer (CIO)*

As enterprises transform the role of technology, the role of the CIO and the IT unit becomes critical to success. No longer can the CIO merely be responsible for the back-office systems or simply be an order taker to the needs and whims of the business. In virtually every successful transformation we have studied, the CIO played a pivotal role. A successful transformation is not just a matter of introducing digital technologies into the enterprise. Many technologies can be easily copied, and they don't provide a competitive advantage. Instead, the transformation's success will rest on the enterprise's ability to integrate, creating a multiproduct, multichannel experience, or a single view of the customer, or services that couple products with data.[12] The CIO is well positioned to lead integration efforts (think of the work done to integrate silos into platforms).

And the difference between effective and ineffective CIOs is a big potential leverage point for the enterprise. On the next pages, we will describe what separates CIOs of top-performing enterprises from their bottom-performing competitors. Our insights come from our survey of more than four hundred CIOs globally.[13] These differences will help explain the opportunities and challenges that CIOs face in a digital economy.

CIOs of top-performing enterprises—with net margins in the top quartile relative to their industry average—spend their time differently than other CIOs do, in three areas:

1. They spend more time with external customers.

2. They obsessively focus on innovation.

3. They are deeply engaged with their executive committees.

Let's examine at each of these action areas.

**Spending more time with external customers.** In 2008, we began asking CIOs to estimate how they spend their time. There has been a significant shift in their time allocation recently. In 2008, the average CIO spent only 10 percent of his or her time engaging with external customers, focused on selling, sharing best practices, and working with the customers to integrate the CIO's enterprise offerings with the customers' systems. By 2015, CIOs had doubled the time spent with external customers to 20 percent, often reducing the time spent running the IT unit and delegating more of that role to others.[14]

CIOs who spend time with customers have firsthand knowledge of the customer pain points and the integration initiatives that will create a better customer experience. This is particularly true for ecosystem drivers and omnichannels in B2B enterprises.

Chris Perretta, chief information and operations officer for the Americas for MUFG Americas Holdings Corporation, reflected, "CIOs naturally need to 'walk in their customers' shoes' to design solutions that deliver value as defined by their customers across a broad customer base without introducing extraordinary levels of complexity and cost."[15]

**Focusing obsessively on innovation.** Virtually every enterprise we talk with is focused on innovation, for good reason: typically, new revenues come from innovation. In our survey, we found that a huge 49 percent of the top-performing enterprises' revenues came from new products introduced in the last three years, compared with just 13 percent in the bottom-performing enterprises. CIOs of top-performing enterprises are obsessed with innovation—those surveyed spend 53 percent of their time on it, in stark contrast to CIOs in the bottom-performing enterprises, who spend 19 percent of their time on innovation. Transforming the experience and then keeping it fresh and appealing to customers requires a constant stream of innovations, and the CIO has the expertise to integrate them.

**Working with executive committees.** The executive committees of top-performing enterprises spend about half of their time— 51 percent—focused on digitally enabled threats and opportunities. This is nearly triple the time spent by the executive committees of bottom-performing enterprises (18 percent), which are more likely to concentrate on operational issues. CIOs of the top-performing enterprises in our survey spend more of their time advising and consulting to the executive committee, for example, presenting to their executive committees at 61 percent of meetings, compared with 46 percent of the bottom performers. The CIO's knowledge of what digital can do for an enterprise needs to be exploited in a transformation. Beyond their general business role as a member of the executive committee on strategy and other roles, CIOs reported three techniques that help their executive committees deal with digital issues. First, CIOs produce a digital dashboard that at one glance identifies problems and value creation enterprise-wide (not just in the IT budget). The use of the dashboard provides confidence and enables efficient executive committee oversight and action if needed.

Reporting regularly on cybersecurity, the second effective technique, includes discussions on both current and potential issues. The third technique is the establishment of clear and simple IT governance and its expansion to digital governance that covers the IoT, automation, data, and all other digital assets in the enterprise. A good test of clear and simple governance is whether each member of the executive committee can describe the decision rights and accountabilities for major decisions like capital investment and architecture.

---

Time spent with customers, a focus on innovation, and working with the executive committee differentiated top-performing CIOs and their enterprises from their bottom-performing competitors. And these three areas are a great place for CIOs and IT units to make a real difference in leading the enterprise toward a successful future in the digital era.

Transformation creates a career fork for most CIOs. If the CIO is one of the leaders of the transformation, their percentage of time on managing enterprise processes is likely to double—specifically focused on simultaneously improving customer experience and increasing operational efficiency through automation—particularly through the creation of reusable digital platforms with exposed APIs. If the CIO isn't one of the leaders of the transformation, then he or she will focus more time on managing IT services, which will expand to include all digital services, like the IoT.

To get an idea of the readiness of the people in your enterprise to tackle a transformation, do the chapter 6 self-assessment. The

---

**CHAPTER 6**

## Self-assessment

How digitally savvy is your board? (1 = Not at all, 10 = Extremely savvy) ☐

How effective is your board in dealing with digital disruption and transformation? (1 = Not at all, 10 = Very effective) ☐

How important is business-model transformation to your CEO and executive committee? (1 = Not at all, 10 = Extremely important) ☐

How important is transforming the workplace to your CEO and executive committee? (1 = Not at all, 10 = Extremely important) ☐

How important is talent development to your CEO and executive committee? (1 = Not at all, 10 = Extremely important) ☐

How influential is your CIO with the executive committee? (1 = Not at all, 10 = Very influential) ☐

How effective is your culture (emphasis on design, test, and learn; evidence-based decision making; agile mindset; partnering; minimum viable products; learning) at making the most of digital? (1 = Not at all effective, 10 = Extremely effective) ☐

How resistant is your organization toward change? (1 = Very resistant and difficult to change, 10 = Very open to change) ☐

How much time does your CIO spend with customers? (1 = No time, 10 = All of his or her time) ☐

How digital is your company, especially in creating services that can be delivered online? (1 = None of our revenues come from digital, 10 = All our revenues come from digital) ☐

**Total** ☐

*Source:* © 2017 MIT Sloan Center for Information Systems Research. Used with permission.

---

average score of top performers on this assessment is 68.[16] How do you compare? If your assessment reveals any individual scores that are significantly lower than the rest (say 5 or lower), you'll know that those areas of leadership should be strengthened.

Next, we conclude the book with some final thoughts on how to make your digital transformation a reality.

## CONCLUSION

# Putting It All Together

Digital disruption and the burgeoning digital era is a wonderful—and critical—opportunity for you as a leader to help reinvent your enterprise. As we've seen throughout this book, it's not a matter of *if* but rather a matter of when and how your business will make the changes necessary to survive and prosper. The most successful enterprises will have to be ambidextrous: both innovating and reducing costs. These successful enterprises will innovate focusing on learning more about their customers and, at the same time, opening up the enterprise boundaries and relying on partners. And they will become more efficient, relentlessly reducing cost every year through simplification and automation. Without that sort of ambidexterity, your company will suffer while startups, enterprises in other industries, and more-agile competitors slice bits off your businesses until there is little left.

As we come to the end of this book, we ask you to return to figure I-2 from the introduction. It will serve a guide for your enterprise to set its course for transformation. Each step in the figure (and the associated chapter) provides a key question you should be able to answer as your company undertakes a digital business transformation. Each chapter's framework will guide you, and the self-assessments will help you understand the urgency of the case for action. Self-assessments are a powerful tool to generate discussion and identify actions that need to be taken. Take a moment to consider the key question for each step in the introduction's figure I-2 and the actions you will take. Let's review these steps together.

## 1. What Is the Digital Threat—and Opportunity?

The first question, on digital threat, sets the stage and helps you and your colleagues identify the case for action and the need for change. Often, senior management team members disagree on their assessments of digital threat. This disagreement can lead to a productive discussion on the definition of terms and can help teams more precisely articulate how they measure threats and their impacts. Such disagreement also can help the senior team understand just how varied employees' views about the digital threat might be, especially in a large enterprise. All this discussion serves the important process of getting everyone in the company on the same page regarding perceived threats and opportunities.

If the senior team determines that a large percentage of the company's revenues is threatened, then the company must act as soon as possible to avoid disruption. Usually that means developing new business models and may entail major organizational surgery, which opens up the opportunity to reinvent the company. During organizational surgery, clear communication becomes paramount. The CEO and other leaders need to share with the entire enterprise the conclusions from their analysis and the steps ahead—articulating the changes to come in areas such as who makes decisions and any changes in the organizational structure and the company culture. Thus, the enterprise builds the consensus that will be needed for the transformation ahead.

## 2. Which Business Model Is Best for Your Enterprise's Future?

The second question prompts you to identify where your enterprise is headed. We've identified four models for generating revenue in the digital economy. We've also found that many large companies will have revenues from not just one but multiple business models. So where are you today, and where do you want to be on the DBM framework? Start thinking about which model or models can let you exploit your current capabilities. But if *all* your current capabilities need strengthening, then it is time for radical reenvisioning—perhaps even to the point of creating a new enterprise or business unit to get you successfully competing in the digital economy. This is a great time to involve the board—transforming the organization is a costly, time-consuming, people-intensive process, and board members will be important allies. An important benefit of identifying your target business model(s) will be that you'll create a common language among the senior executives and employees about what is possible—and where the enterprise is going on its digital business transformation.

## 3. What Is Your Digital Competitive Advantage?

Now that you know where you want to go on the DBM framework, the next part of the process requires a fairly hard-headed look at how good your company is at each of the three sources of competitive advantage in a digital economy: content, customer experience, and platforms. If your company faces a significant threat of disruption, most likely you don't have a competitive advantage in one of those areas. You will therefore need to decide which area will be your source of competitive advantage, and you'll create a road map to build and strengthen that advantage. Again, a key benefit of this process is the creation of a common language and clarity about the destination and capabilities needed for getting there.

## 4. How Will You Connect Using Mobile and the Internet of Things?

Digital technologies come in many forms and will increase in variety and impact over time. Two of the most important are mobile and the internet of things (IoT). Mobile is unprecedented in its ability to allow your company to connect and interact with your customers, anytime and anywhere. The IoT allows you to develop added services for your customers and gives insights on how they are using your products. These two technologies together create the potential for customers to (automatically) get in touch with you and for you to respond (automatically), all leading to much better services and a deeper understanding of your customer. How your company will use these two technologies is driven by your answers to the previous two questions: which DBM (or DBMs) will serve your enterprise best, and what is (or are) your source (or sources) of competitive advantage? Successful enterprises will find ways to use mobile and the IoT to transform themselves. But first you have to integrate mobile and digitally managed assets (i.e., the IoT) into your company's capabilities.

### 5. Do You Have the Crucial Capabilities to Reinvent the Enterprise?

Once you have established the need for transformation, figured out how to make money in the future, and identified your source or sources of competitive advantage, you need to start obtaining options (investing) and otherwise preparing for the necessary organizational changes to successfully implement the new business model or models. We identified eight key capabilities for reinventing your enterprise.

Again, an important initial step is an honest conversation, first among the senior executives and then later with participants across the company, about the company's current strengths and weaknesses in each of the eight capabilities. Then you'll need to build capability programs that include significant investments in skills, technology, culture, and partnerships. Here, senior management must be clear about the business model and the choices around the sources of competitive advantage. These choices will drive the amount of investment and improvement required in each key capability. The good news is that whichever business models and sources of competitive advantage you choose, investing in the eight capabilities will help drive success. The bad news is that becoming world-class in any of these eight capabilities—let alone all of them—is not easy and requires constant, long-term attention from the whole enterprise, probably for many years to come.

## 6. *Do You Have the Leadership to Make Your Transformation Happen?*

Leadership is important—no kidding! But it turns out that, in digital business transformation, company leaders have at least two jobs: (1) focusing the organization on new business models and new sources of competitive advantage and (2) changing the culture so that the company will not only achieve the targets but also continue to adapt in the next decade and more. We think leading a transformation is a core enterprise skill that leaders need to develop now and in the future.

Leaders can focus the company by setting goals and then measuring progress toward those goals and by managing investments, particularly innovation investments that support movement toward new business models. One of the most helpful ways to measure progress is to identify, using your chosen model or models from the DBM framework, the current and three-year targets for revenue percentages and profit margins. Then each month, track the progress from where you are today to where you need to be. But do avoid a wasteful practice that we've seen in some companies attempting innovation—senior executives who encourage "a thousand flowers to bloom" rather than target innovation to the strategic decisions already made about business models and sources of competitive advantage.

Leading cultural change can come in many forms but often includes several helpful practices. As a leader, you can improve the digital expertise of everybody in the enterprise through education and project work. You can get more people involved in innovation (a good target is more than 50 percent of your employees, as we saw DBS achieved). You can also create a more evidence-based culture by using data more effectively. And you can become better at partnerships both through your people (e.g., collaboration) and through your systems (e.g., APIs).

Ensuring that your company has the right person leading the transformation is paramount. For example, companies that choose platforms as their number one source of competitive advantage (i.e., modular producers on the DBM framework) often ask the CIO to lead the transformation. Companies that identify customer experience as their primary source of competitive advantage (i.e., omnichannels) often ask the chief experience officer or the chief marketing officer to lead the transformation. Companies that choose content as their main competitive advantage (i.e., suppliers) often ask product owners and product-innovation teams to lead. And ecosystem drivers need a leader who can integrate all three sources of competitive advantage, perhaps the chief operating officer or CEO.

---

The research and writing we've done for this book has been a rich and enjoyable learning experience—first learning what is important to leaders for transformation and then watching as they put our findings into action, providing real-time feedback on what's working and what isn't.

For the leaders we studied, none of their transformations were easy. Digital business transformation is hard work. Successful transformation requires leaders to build a common understanding of the threats and to identify where the company is going; to communicate that vision to the entire company; and to make the hard choices about decision rights and organizational restructuring. Leaders must also be vigilant about ensuring that the company's investments in capabilities and innovation reflect their decisions about which DBM (or DBMs) and sources of competitive advantage to target. All this work must be done while the leaders are developing the leadership and talent necessary to carry out the changes. Finally, leaders have to create the culture they need, making sure things like incentives, training, investments, and hiring practices support that cultural vision, while measuring results and holding the right people accountable.

These steps present a profound challenge, to be sure. But the rewards are significant, both personally for leaders and for the enterprise. The digital era presents businesses with a rare and exciting opportunity—it's not often that leaders of an enterprise get to reinvent the business. Now it's your turn. What actions will you and your colleagues take today that will make the difference?

# NOTES

## Introduction

1. R. Ghose et al., "Digital Disruption—Revisited," *Citi GPS: Global Perspectives & Solutions*, January 2017.

2. R. Ghose et al., "Digital Disruption: How FinTech is Forcing Banking to a Tipping Point," *Citi GPS: Global Perspectives & Solutions*, March 2016.

3. Stephen Gandel, "Here's How Citigroup Is Embracing the 'Fintech' Revolution," *Fortune*, June 27, 2016, http://fortune.com/citigroup-fintech.

4. Nick Wingfield, "Amazon Finds a Fit in Apparel," *New York Times*, May 1, 2017.

5. P. Weill and S. L. Woerner, "Optimizing Your Digital Business Model," *MIT Sloan Management Review* (spring 2013), reprint 54322.

6. P. Weill and S. L. Woerner, "Working with Your Board on Digital Disruption," *MIT CISR Briefing* 15, no. 4 (April 2015). We began the board research in 2014 (hereafter cited as Weill and Woerner, "Boards [2014]") by interviewing nine board members in several countries to learn about the digital issues and challenges board members face. We then conducted a survey that eighty-three board members answered. We asked a variety of questions to assess effective practices that boards used for dealing with digital disruption. We also asked about the effective relationships that help the boards understand how to use digital technologies successfully and the extent to which digitization was affecting their companies.

We conducted three in-depth case studies, two of them with Abbie Lundberg. We interviewed the CIO at Tenet Health about the CIO-board relationship, and we interviewed several senior executives and at least one board member at Emerson Electric and Principal Financial about the role of the board in helping the company deal with digital disruption. Finally, we have held workshops with more than twelve large company boards.

7. The research described in this chapter is primarily drawn from four studies:

### Digital Business Models (2011–2013)

We started this research (hereafter cited as Weill and Woerner, "Digital Business Models [2011–2013]") by creating a framework that drew on previous research and many conversations with CIOs and other senior leaders about the challenges of operating in a more-digital world. We designed a survey to validate the framework, and 118 companies responded. We supplemented this survey data with financial company performance data from the Compustat database for statistical analyses. We measured the effectiveness of a company's content, customer experience, and platform by averaging the answers to questions about different aspects of each construct (nine questions about content; nine about customer experience, and eight about platform). We also collected detailed secondary data on companies, including news reports and other publicly available information. To collect data for the LexisNexis case study, we conducted structured interviews with six of the company's most senior executives. Data for the USAA case was drawn from public sources, senior executive presentations, and a MIT Sloan School of Management's Center for Information Systems Research (MIT CISR) case study (Jeanne W. Ross and Cynthia M. Beath, "USAA: Organizing for Innovation and Superior Customer Services," working paper 382, MIT CISR, Cambridge, MA, December 2010). We also completed a detailed case study of Banco do Brasil and case vignettes from public sources on Apple, Bloomberg, Commonwealth Bank of Australia, and Netflix. Finally, to refine the work, we shared our analysis with executives in the companies we studied and in workshops in Boston, Mumbai, Paris, São Paulo, Seattle, Singapore, and Sydney, with executives experienced in transforming their enterprises to succeed in a digital environment.

The authors would like to acknowledge that important contributions to this research came from Jeanne Ross, Peter Reynolds, Michele Vivona, and John Sviokla.

### The Next Generation Enterprise (2012–2016)

We began this research (hereafter cited as Weill and Woerner, "Next-Generation Enterprise [2012–2016]"), focused on how organizations were going to thrive in the digital economy, in March 2012 with a series of virtual roundtables with senior executives from thirteen large corporations across a variety of industries. We then followed up with an in-person roundtable with executives from seventeen companies. We posed the following question: "Describe a breakthrough organizational change enabled by digitization where your company has significantly changed the way you operate with early indications of good results." Participants described seventy-seven initiatives, which we classified by types of transformation. We found that many of the companies were seeking to transform on two dimensions: to know more about their end customers and to operate in an increasingly digital ecosystem where they become a destination to solve a customer's life or business need with products and services from their company, from complementors, and sometimes from competitors. These two dimensions became the axes of the two-by-two framework with four digital business models: supplier, omnichannel, modular producer, and ecosystem driver.

To understand best practices and the impact of these business models on financial performance, we surveyed two groups of senior executives: clients of Gartner Inc. (93 participants) and companies associated with the MIT CISR (101 participants). We asked participants to rate a variety of organization practices and performance measures and to describe a significant breakthrough initiative; we received an additional 67 descriptions (for a total of 144).

To identify top performers, we collected self-reported company data on net profit margins and revenue growth. To check the accuracy of the self-reported data, we added actual 2013 financial performance from Onesource.com (now Avention.com). Self-reported net profit margin and revenue correlated significantly with actual net profit margin and revenue growth. Financial measures were then adjusted by industry. We tested a series of hypotheses to understand best practices for each type of business. We did an exemplar case study for each quadrant (using P&G as the supplier, Woolworths as the omnichannel business, PayPal as the modular producer, and Aetna as the ecosystem driver).

Finally, we created a series of case studies—on Aetna, BBVA, and mBank—examining how a company moves from one quadrant to another. We have conducted over fifty workshops on this material with senior executives and boards of directors.

### Digital Disruption (2014–2016)

We began our investigation (hereafter cited as Weill and Woerner, "Digital Disruption [2014–2016]") of how large enterprises were facing digital disruption with a survey, which was answered by 413 executives. We asked about the level of digital threat, the drivers of digital threat, digital investment allocations, effective practices to deal with digital disruption, and the role of the executive committee.

For companies that identified themselves on the survey, we added financial data and industry averages from Onesource.com and Factiva.com. Self-reported net profit margin correlated significantly with actual net profit margin, so we used self-reported net profit margin, adjusted for industry, as our financial performance variable. We used a variety of statistical methods—correlations, ANOVAs, and regression analyses—and results reported are significant.

We completed several case studies, on BBVA, Schneider Electric, and DBS Bank. In these cases, we interviewed a number of senior executives and compiled both company and public documents. To get at specific aspects of digital disruption, we asked executives from Microsoft, Fairfax Media, Principal Financial, and CIBC for written reactions.

### Mobile Apps (2013–2014)

To understand how companies were using and generating value from customer mobile apps, we conducted a survey and five case studies (Dunkin' Donuts, iGaranti, Johnson & Johnson, Westpac, and Woolworths). In the case studies, we typically interviewed three or four people in each company and analyzed documents, the mobile app, and firm performance. We received 334 surveys from responses from executives knowledgeable about their companies' mobile strategy. We asked respondents to answer the survey with their most popular customer mobile app in mind. We assessed mobile investment allocation, mobile strategy, stakeholders involved, effectiveness of the app, technical and data capabilities of the app, and reuse. In addition, we asked respondents to self-report financial and enterprise performance information.

For companies that identified themselves on the survey, we added financial data and industry averages from Onesource.com. Self-reported net profit margin correlated significantly with actual net profit margin, so we used self-reported net profit margin, adjusted for industry, as our financial performance variable. Results reported are significant in regression analyses.

8. M. E. Porter, *Competitive Strategy* (New York: Free Press, 1980).

9. Commonwealth Bank of Australia, "Want to Know If You Can Afford the Home You Love? We've Got the Key," web page about property-appraisal app, accessed October 22, 2017, www.commbank.com.au/personal/home-loans/commbank-property-app.html.

10. Aetna introduced this vision in 2014 (see Aetna Foundation, "Aetna Releases Aetna Story 2014: Building a Healthier World," press release, April 21, 2014, http://news.aetnafoundation.org/press-release/aetna-releases-aetna-story-2014-building-healthier-world). Financial performance comparisons are from Onesource.com and Factiva.com.

11. Seven & i Holdings Co., Ltd., 2016 Annual Report, 31; and Onesource.com.

12. A. R. Sorkin, "Why Uber Might Well Be Worth $18 Billion," *New York Times*, June 10, 2014, B1.

13. A. Karunakaran, J. G. Mooney, and J. W. Ross, "Accelerating Digital Platform Deployment Using the Cloud: A Case Study of Schneider Electric's 'Bridge Front Office' Program," working paper 399, MIT CISR, Cambridge, MA, January 2015.

14. Paul Grey, "(2015) How Many Products Does Amazon Sell?," *ExportX*, December 11, 2015, https://export-x.com/2015/12/11/how-many-products-does-amazon-sell-2015.

15. Connie Chan, "When One App Rules Them All: The Case of WeChat and Mobile in China," Andreessen Horowitz web page, August 6, 2015, http://a16z.com/2015/08/06/wechat-china-mobile-first.

16. USAA, "And the Winner Is: USAA Ranks High in Customer Service, Loyalty," *USAA News* Center, August 8, 2016, https://communities.usaa.com/t5/Inside-the-Mission/And-the-Winner-Is-USAA-Ranks-High-in-Customer-Service-Loyalty/ba-p/98448.

17. M. Ravindranath, "Cisco CEO at CES 2014: Internet of Things Is a $19 Trillion Opportunity," *Washington Post*, January 8, 2014.

## Chapter 1

1. T. Eistert et al., "Banking in a Digital World," A. T. Kearney and Efma research report, 2013, www.atkearney.de/documents/856314/3998533/Banking+in+a+digital+world.pdf.

2. "The Digital Disruption in Banking," *2014 North American Consumer Digital Banking Survey*, www.accenture.com/us-en/~/media/Accenture/Conversion-Assets/DotCom/Documents/Global/PDF/Industries_5/Accenture-2014-NA-Consumer-Digital-Banking-Survey.pdf.

3. Much of the material on BBVA in this book is based on discussions with Chairman Francisco González and other BBVA executives, company materials provided to MIT CISR, and information from the company website. The descriptions of BBVA's transformation have been approved by the company and is used with their permission.

4. I. Boudway and M. Chafkin, "ESPN Has Seen the Future of TV and They're Not Really Into It," *Bloomberg Businessweek*, March 30, 2017, www.bloomberg.com/news/features/2017-03-30/espn-has-seen-the-future-of-tv-and-they-re-not-really-into-it.

5. D. Kerr, "Digital Banking: BBVA's González—the Digital Banker," *Euromoney*, September 11, 2014, www.euromoney.com/Article/3379655/Digital-banking-BBVAs-GonzlezThe-digital-banker.html.

6. Ibid.

7. BBVA, "BBVA Acquires 14.89% of Garanti from Dogus, Strengthening Growth Profile," BBVA, October 9, 2015, www.bbva.com/en/bbva-acquires-14-89-of-garanti-from-dogus-strengthening-growth-profile.

8. P. Weill and S. L. Woerner, "Creating Great Mobile Apps for Customers: Effective Practice and iGaranti's Story," *MIT CISR Briefing* 15, no. 5 (May 2015).

9. Garanti BBVA Group, "Investor Relations," accessed October 22, 2017, www.garantiinvestorrelations.com/en/financial-information/detay/Garanti-in-Brief/252/510/0.

10. Kerr, "Digital Banking: BBVA's González—the Digital Banker."

11. BBVA, "Francisco González: "We Are Building the Best Digital Bank of the 21st Century," BBVA web page, March 13, 2015, www.bbva.com/en/francisco-gonzalez-we-are-building-the-best-digital-bank-of-the-21st-century.

12. P. Weill and S. L. Woerner, "Is Your Company a Digital Leader or Digital Laggard?," *MIT CISR Briefing* 17, no. 3 (March 2017).

13. Financials and other information from Onesource.com, Factiva.com, and the company websites.

## Chapter 2

1. For information about TripAdvisor, see "About TripAdvisor" log files, Q3 2017, https://tripadvisor.mediaroom.com/us-about-us.

2. Several parts of this chapter draw on P. Weill and S. L. Woerner, "Thriving in an Increasingly Digital Ecosystem," *MIT Sloan Management Review* 56, no. 4 (summer 2015), reprint 56417.

3. The research in this chapter is drawn primarily from Weill and Woerner, "Next-Generation Enterprise (2012–2016).

4.  BloomReach, "Amazon Grabs 55 Percent of Consumers' First Product Search, Set to Dominate 2016 Holiday Shopping," *PRNewsire*, September 27, 2016.

5.  James B. Stewart, "Walmart Plays Catch-Up with Amazon," *New York Times*, October 23, 2015.

6.  Quoted in Wikipedia, s.v. "William Gibson," last modified July 2, 2017, https://en.wikiquote.org/wiki/William_Gibson.

7.  For 2016 figures, see Reuters, "Amazon's Third-Party Sellers Had Record-Breaking Sales in 2016," *Fortune*, January 4, 2017, http://fortune.com/2017/01/04/amazon-marketplace-sales. For 2014 and 2015, see L. Rao, "This Lesser-Known Amazon Business Is Growing Fast," *Fortune*, January 5, 2016, http://fortune.com/2016/01/05/amazon-sellers-holidays.

8.  Commonwealth Bank of Australia, "Want to Know If You Can Afford the Home You Love? We've Got the Key," web page about property-appraisal app, accessed October 22, 2017, www.commbank.com.au/personal/home-loans/commbank-property-app.html.

9.  Cream, "Property Guide App," accessed October 22, 2017, www.creamglobal.com/17798/24522/property-guide-app.

10.  Weill and Woerner, "Next-Generation Enterprise (2012–2016)."

11.  The capabilities of an ecosystem-driver model are drawn from research done in partnership with Harvey Nash. See S. L. Woerner and P. Weill, "Digital Ecosystem Models Are Consolidating—Move Quickly," special report in *Navigating Uncertainty: CIO Survey 2017* (Harvey Nash/KPMG, 2017), 53, https://assets.kpmg.com/content/dam/kpmg/xx/pdf/2017/07/harvey-nash-kpmg-cio-survey-2017.pdf.

12.  Jeanne W. Ross and Cynthia M. Beath, "USAA: Organizing for Innovation and Superior Customer Service," working paper 382, MIT CISR, Cambridge, MA, December 2010; Martin Mocker and Jeanne W. Ross, "USAA: Capturing Value from Complexity," working paper 389, MIT CISR, Cambridge, MA, March 2013.

13.  Satmetrix, "U.S. Consumer 2016: Net Promoter Benchmarks at a Glance," Satmetrix, 2016, http://info.satmetrix.com/hubfs/2016-nps-b2c-benchmark-infographic.pdf?t=1467330932188). The NPS was the percentage of customers who are promoters minus the percentage who are detractors. Scores range from –100 to +100.

14.  Data from 194 enterprises from MIT CISR 2013 Ecosystem Survey and MIT CISR-Gartner 2013 Ecosystem Survey (hereafter cited as "MIT CISR-Gartner 2013 Ecosystem Survey"). Statistically significant regression analysis of ninety-three large enterprises (revenues greater than $1 billion): the net margin relative to competitors is predicted by the percentage of revenues from ecosystems and the level of customer knowledge (a seven-item measure).

15. Data from 194 enterprises from MIT CISR 2013 Ecosystem Survey and MIT CISR-Gartner 2013 Ecosystem Survey. Self-reported net profit margin correlates to actual net profit margin at $p < 0.05$ and self-reported revenue growth correlates to actual revenue growth at $p < 0.09$. Financial measures are relative to industry. Customer experience and time to market were assessed relative to competitors. All measures were transformed to a 0–100 percent scale. Differences between models for each measure are significant at $p < 0.05$.

16. A. Nag and J. McGeever, "Foreign Exchange, the World's Biggest Market, Is Shrinking," Reuters, February 11, 2016, www.reuters.com/article/us-global-fx-peaktrading-idUSKCN0VK1UD.

# Chapter 3

1. ClickFox Mobile Apps Customer Survey, October 2011 (650 participants). See Joe Brockmeier, "Infographic: Mobile Apps and Customer Engagement," ReadWrite, November 9, 2011, https://readwrite.com/2011/11/09/infographic-mobile-apps-and-cu/. That same survey also found that 78 percent of the sample reported using apps to interact with companies with which they do business, like banks and retailers.

2. comScore, Inc., "The 2016 U.S. Mobile App Report," white paper, comScore, September 13, 2016, www.comscore.com/Insights/Presentations-and-Whitepapers/2016/The-2016-US-Mobile-App-Report.

3. WBR Digital, "Mobile First Mentality: Turning Browsers into Buyers," *Digital Doughnut*, December 12, 2016, www.digitaldoughnut.com/resources/2017/wbr-digital/report-mobile-first-mentality.

4. This chapter draws from Weill and Woerner, "Digital Business Models (2011–2013)." Other important background research includes P. Weill and M. Vitale, *Place to Space: Migrating to eBusiness Models* (Boston: Harvard Business School Press, 2001); and J. Rayport and J. Sviokla, "Managing in the Marketspace," *Harvard Business Review*, November–December 1994, 141–150. Portions of this research were published in P. Weill and S. L. Woerner, "Optimizing Your Digital Business Model," *Sloan Management Review*, spring 2013.

5. These relationships are all statistically significant in a regression equation in our sample of 118 companies, controlling for industry and using multiple measures for content, customer experience, and platforms.

6. For more on platforms, see P. Weill and J. W. Ross, *IT Savvy: What Top Executives Must Know to Go from Pain to Gain* (Boston: Harvard Business School Press, 2009).

7. For one of the earliest and most insightful discussions of this move from place to space, see J. F. Rayport and J. Sviokla, "Managing in the Marketspace."

8. J. B. Stewart, "Netflix Looks Back on Its Near-Death Spiral," *New York Times*, April 26, 2013.

9. R. Hastings, "An Explanation and Some Reflections," Netflix company blog, September 18, 2011, https://media.netflix.com/en/company-blog/ an-explanation-and-some-reflections.

10. Statistica, "Number of Netflix Streaming Subscribers Worldwide from 3rd Quarter 2011 to 1st Quarter 2017 (in Millions)," *Statista: The Statistics Portal*, accessed June 15, 2017, www.statista.com/statistics/250934/quarterly- number-of-netflix-streaming-subscribers-worldwide.

11. See TripAdvisor Q3 2017 Results, http://files.shareholder.com/ downloads/AMDA-MMXS5/5571857298x0x962899/81A73905-36F6-44E9- B8BC-7D92320C3A22/TRIP_Q3_2017_Investor_Presentation.pdf.

12. Ibid.

13. Paul Sawers, "TripAdvisor Acquires HouseTrip As Home-Rental Market Consolidates," *Venture Beat*, April 28, 2016, http://venturebeat.com/2016/04/28/ tripadvisor-acquires-housetrip-as-home-rental-market-consolidates.

14. Steve Kaufer, "TripAdvisor CEO: What's Ahead After 100M Mile- stone," interview by Adrienne Mitchell, *MarketWatch Radio*, March 18, 2018, www.marketwatch.com/story/tripadvisor-ceo-whats-ahead-after-100m- milestone-2013-03-18-710710.

15. Financial numbers and ratios are from Onesource.com and Factiva.com.

16. DBS material is from S. K. Sia, P. Weill, and C. Soh, "DBS Bank: Developing Tech and Ops Capabilities for Pan-Asian Growth," working paper 391, MIT CISR, Cambridge, MA, August 2013; K. Dery, I. M. Sebas- tian, and N. van der Meulen, "Building Value from the Digital Workplace," *MIT CISR Briefing* 16, no. 9 (September 2106); DBS home page, www.dbs. com; and Onesource.com for financial data.

17. Adam Richardson, "Using Customer Journey Maps to Improve Customer Experience," *Harvard Business Review*, November 15, 2010, https://hbr.org/2010/11/using-customer-journey-maps-to.

18. "Banking without branches, DBS digibank India gains 1m customers in a year," DBS Innovates blog, June 8, 2017, https://www.dbs.com/innovation/ dbs-innovates/banking-without-branches-dbs-digibank-india-gains-1m- customers-in-a-year.html.

19. Much of the information on Commonwealth Bank of Australia comes from Peter Reynolds, et al., "Design Your Platform for Business Agility and Performance," *MIT CISR Briefing* 16, no. 2 (February 2016; revised

March 2016). For CBA's tenth-largest size, see "World's Largest Banks 2017," www.relbanks.com/worlds-top-banks/market-cap.

20. For numbers of employees and branches, see Commonwealth Bank of Australia, "Debt Investor Update for the Half Year Ended 31 December 2016," February 15, 2017, www.commbank.com.au/content/dam/commbank/about-us/group-funding/articles/debt-investor-update-hy2017.pdf. For number of digital customers, see Commonwealth Bank of Australia, "20 Years of Digital Banking Innovation at CommBank," press release, June 6, 2017, www.commbank.com.au/guidance/newsroom/20-years-of-digital-banking-innovation-201706.html.

21. Pat McConnell, "Banking Outlook: Threats from Technology, Burst of Housing Bubble, End of Mining Boom," *The Conversation*, March 13, 2016, https://theconversation.com/banking-outlookthreats-from-technology-burst-of-housing-bubbleend- of-mining-boom-55627.

22. The retail bank cost-to-income ratio was reduced from 54.7 to 47.2 percent, and the gap between CBA and its top-rated peer had closed, decreasing from 12.5 to 7.8 percent.

23. McConnell, "Banking Outlook," 3.

24. Ibid.

25. James Eyers, "Commonwealth Bank Technology Investment to Keep Fintech on Backfoot," *Australian Financial Review*, August 17, 2015, www.afr.com/ business/banking-and-finance/commonwealth-bank-technology-investment-tokeep-fintech-on-backfoot-20150815-gizysc#ixzz43JiCw6J4%C2%A0.

26. The Editors of *Inc.*, "*Inc.* 5000 2015: The Full List: Our Annual Ranking of the Fastest-Growing Private Companies in America," *Inc.*, accessed October 22, 2017, www.inc.com/inc5000/list/2015.

27. BMW Group, "Mobility Is Becoming Tailor-Made," *Future Views*, accessed October 22, 2017, www.bmwgroup.com/en/next100/futureviews/tailor-made.html.

28. Our research on LexisNexis began in 2011 in our collaboration with Michele Vivona and ten of her colleagues and included six interviews. See, for example, S. L. Woerner, P. Weill, and M. Vivona, "How LexisNexis Strengthened Its Digital Business Model," *MIT CISR Briefing* 12, no. 1 (January 2012). We miss you, Michele, and hope you are resting in peace. You were taken way too early from all of us.

29. LexisNexis, "LexisNexis Honored as a 2017 Achievement in Customer Excellence Award Winner," *LexisNexis Newsroom*, May 16, 2017, www.lexisnexis.com/en-us/about-us/media/press-release.page?id=1494929458278350&y=2017.

30. Content, platforms, and customer-experience scores are from the MIT CISR 2010 Digital Business Models Survey (130 participants). A top performer was an enterprise with above-median revenue growth, adjusted for industry. Platforms were measured with five questions, content with six, and customer experience with seven. We calculated the score for top performers on each measure and converted the scores to a 1–10 scale.

## Chapter 4

1. The research in this chapter is drawn primarily from two studies from Weill and Woerner, "Mobile Apps (2013–2014)"; and from the following study we conducted.

### Internet of Things (2015)

To investigate how the internet of things (IoT) could be used to change an enterprise's business model, we ran a survey, interviewed executives in five companies, and conducted two case studies. For one case study, Flex, we held interviews with four senior executives and analyzed various documents. We used several public sources to assemble the Schindler case. Respondents from 413 enterprises answered the survey.

For companies that identified themselves in the survey, we added financial data and industry averages from Onesource.com and Factiva. com. Self-reported net margin correlated significantly with actual net margin, so we used self-reported net margin, adjusted for industry, as our financial performance variable. Results reported are significant in regression analysis.

2. comScore, "The 2017 U.S. Mobile App Report," https://www. comscore.com/Insights/Presentations-and-Whitepapers/2017/The-2017-US-Mobile-App-Report.

3. eMarketer, "Growth of Time Spent on Mobile Devices Slows," *Media Buying* (eMarketer blog), October 7, 2015, www.emarketer.com/Article/Growth-of-Time-Spent-on-Mobile-Devices-Slows/1013072.

4. This section draws heavily on P. Weill and S. L. Woerner, "Mobile Customer App Engagement Pays Off," *European Business Review*, November–December 2015.

5. Sarah Perez, "Pokémon Go's Retention Rates, Average Revenue Per User Are Double the Industry Average," *TechCrunch*, July 15, 2016, https:// techcrunch.com/2016/07/15/pokemon-gos-retention-rates-average-revenue-

per-user-are-double-the-industry-average; Paul Tassi, "Firm Estimates 'Pokémon GO' Has 7.5M Downloads, $1.6M Daily Revenue in US Alone," *Forbes*, July 11, 2016, www.forbes.com/sites/insertcoin/2016/07/11/firm-estimates-pokemon-go-has-7-5m-downloads-1-6m-daily-revenue-in-us-alone.

6. Interviews with Garanti senior management, Garanti's documents, and Garanti website.

7. Jason Murphy, "What Woolworths Needs to Do to Fight Back," *News.com.au*, July 26, 2016, www.news.com.au/finance/business/retail/is-woolworths-at-risk-of-being-killed-by-german-giants/news-story/32fddb1ca6925658a7e620357a8633a0; C. Wahlquist, "Amazon Expands in Australia and Plans Big Warehouse," *Guardian* (London), April 19, 2017.

18. Woolworths, "A Faster Pick Up Is a Tap Away," Woolworths (Australia) web page, accessed October 22, 2017, www.woolworths.com.au/Shop/Discover/about-us/woolworths-app?name=woolworths-app-woolworths-app&cardId=141.

9. Longitudinal Economic Study Series, IRI AttitudeLink, n = 1,000+ shoppers, CPG Purchase Decisions, IRI, 2009, cited in Chris O'Neill, "Three Predictions for the Future of Retail & Brand Marketing," *Google*, May 12, 2011, www.nielsen.com/content/dam/c360/canada/We-re-in-a-Digital-Revolution-Google.pdf, 13.

10. NPS = percentage of promoters – percentage of detractors. Promoters are loyal enthusiasts who will keep buying and will refer others to your site. Detractors are unhappy customers who can damage your brand and impede growth (www.netpromoter.com/np/calculate.jsp).

11. Roy Morgan Research, "Mobile Banking Keeps Customers Happy but Home Loans Are Still Dragging Satisfaction Levels Down," article 7100, Roy Morgan Research, Melbourne, Victoria, January 4, 2017, www.roymorgan.com/findings/7100-mobile-banking-keeps-customers-happy-but-home-loans-dragging-satisfaction-down-201701041049.

12. For more information on this increasing spiral of customer mobile app engagement, see P. Weill and S. L. Woerner, "Creating Great Mobile Apps for Customers: Effective Practice and iGaranti's Story," *MIT CISR Briefing* 15, no. 5 (May 2015).

13. Manyika et al., "Unlocking the Potential of the Internet of Things," *McKinsey Global Institute Report*, June 2015.

14. BI Intelligence, "Will the Internet of Things Be Bigger Than the Industrial Revolution?" *Business Insider: Innovation*, August 17, 2016, www.businessinsider.com/iot-ecosystem-internet-of-things-predictions-and-business-potential-2016-7. GE estimates that there will be fifty billion connected devices by 2020.

15. The case study of Flex draws on our interviews with several senior enterprise executives; and Jeannine Sargent, "2015 Investor and Analyst Day: Connecting the Dots," New York, NY, May 2015, https://s21.q4cdn. com/490720384/files/doc_events/2015/Jeannine_Sargeant.pdf; and flex.com (previously Flextronics.com) and is used with permission.

16. A. Lashinsky, "Why Flex Is Going Beyond Its Manufacturing Roots," *Forbes*, October 22, 2015.

17. Wikipedia, s.v. "Center of excellence," last updated July 28, 2017, https://en.wikipedia.org/wiki/Center_of_excellence, notes: "A center of excellence (CoE) is a team, a shared facility or an entity that provides leadership, best practices, research, support and/or training for a focus area."

18. Schindler case draws on Ina M. Sebastian and Jeanne W. Ross, "The Schindler Group: Driving Innovative Services and Integration with Schindler Digital Business AG" *MIT CISR Vignette*, April 2016, 2; Schindler, "Vision and Values," accessed November 16, 2017, https://www.schindler.com/au/ internet/en/about-us/vision-and-values.html; Schindler, "Schindler Wins MIT Sloan CIO Leadership Award 2015," press release, Schindler, May 21, 2015, www.schindler.com/com/internet/en/media/press-releases-english/press-releases-2015/schindler-wins-mit-sloan-cio-leadership-award-2015.html; Schindler, "Schindler Teams Up with Apple," Schindler, accessed November 3, 2017, www.schindler.com/com/internet/en/ mobility-solutions/success-stories/technology-in-schindler/collaboration-with-apple.html; Schindler 2104 Annual Report, 5; Mary K. Pratt, "CIO Is Pushing the Right Buttons," *CIO from IDG*, October 30, 2015, www.cio. com/article/2993292/big-data/cio-is-pushing-the-right-buttons.html.

19. *Forbes* named Schindler to its 100 Most Innovative Enterprises list in 2011, 2012, and 2013. The German newspaper *Handelsblatt*, along with University of St. Gallen and Capgemini, honored Schindler with the Digital Business Innovation Award in 2015 (Schindler, "Schindler Wins Digital Business Innovation Award 2015," press release, Schindler, February 2, 2015, www.schindler.com/com/internet/en/media/press-releases-english/press-releases-2015/schindler-wins-digital-business-innovation-award-2015.html).

20. The thirty thousand figure is drawn from Schindler, "East Meets West," *Next Floor* (blog), accessed November 3, 2017, www.schindler.com/ content/dam/web/us/PDFs/next-floor/icc.pdf.

21. For more information, see Wikipedia, s.v. "Minimum viable product," last updated November 2, 2017, https://en.wikipedia.org/wiki/Minimum_ viable_product.

22. Stock chart downloaded on June 18, 2017 from Google Finance, www.google.com/finance?chdnp=1&chdd=1&chds=1&chdv=1&chvs= maximized&chdeh=0&chfdeh=0&chdet=1497817415497&chddm=

992749&chls=IntervalBasedLine&cmpto=INDEXSP:.INX&cmptdms=
0&q=NYSE:GE&&fct=big&ei=OuFGWdiGEI2TeYbakpgI.

23. Shareholders' Letter, GE 2016 Annual Report.

24. J. Gertner, "Behind GE's Vision for the Industrial Internet of Things,"
*Fast Company*, June 18, 2014, www.fastcompany.com/3031272/can-jeff-
immelt-really-make-the-world-1-better.

25. GE, "Predix: The Industrial Internet Platform," *GE Digital*,
March 2016, www.ge.com/digital/sites/default/files/predix-platform-brief-ge-
digital.pdf.

26. Wikipedia, s.v. "General Electric," last updated November 3, 2017,
https://en.wikipedia.org/wiki/General_Electric.

27. J. Zorthian, "General Electric Wants to Sell the Lighting Business It
Helped Pioneer 125 Years Ago," *Fortune*, April 6, 2017, http://fortune.com/
2017/04/06/ge-selling-lighting-business.

28. C. Woodward, "General Electric Focuses on Tech in Its Talent Hunt,"
*Boston Globe*, June 12, 2016.

29. GE, "Predix."

30. The 2012 description of what Target could predict with its customer
data was an eye-opener for most. See C. Duhigg, "How Companies Learn
Your Secrets," *New York Times Magazine*, February 16, 2012.

31. B. H. Wixom and L. M. Markus, "To Develop Acceptable Data Use,
Build Company Norms," *MIT CISR Research Briefing* 17, no. 4 (April 2017).

32. S. M. Watson, "If Customers Knew How You Would Use Their Data,
Would They Call It Creepy?" *Harvard Business Review*, April 29, 2014.

33. Mobile readiness scores are from the MIT CISR 2013 Mobile Apps
Survey (334 participants). Top performers were the top quartile of net profit
margin, adjusted for industry. IoT commitment scores are from the MIT CISR
2015 Digital Disruption Survey (413 participants). Top performers are the top
quartile of net profit margin, adjusted for industry by subtracting the industry average. All differences are significant at $p < 0.05$. Scores for each question
have been converted to a 1–10 scale.

## Chapter 5

1. We are borrowing a wonderful concept from James A. Belasco,
*Teaching the Elephant to Dance: The Manager's Guide to Empowering
Change* (New York: Crown, 1990).

2. The research that is the basis for this chapter comes from two studies,
Weill and Woerner, "Next-Generation Enterprise (2012–2016)"; and Weill and
Woerner, "Digital Disruption (2014–2016)."

3. MIT CISR-Gartner 2013 Ecosystem Survey of ninety-three participants. In a statistically significant regression analysis of large firms (revenues greater than $1 billion), the net profit margin relative to competitors is predicted by the percentage of revenues from ecosystems and the level of customer knowledge, measured by seven items such as "To what extent does your enterprise know the identity of the most important end customers of your products or services?"

4. As mentioned in chapter 3, our research on LexisNexis began in 2011 in our work with Michele Vivona and her colleagues. For more details, see S. L. Woerner, P. Weill, and M. Vivona, "How LexisNexis Strengthened Its Digital Business Model," *MIT CISR Briefing* 12, no. 1 (January 2012).

5. The material on Canadian Imperial Bank of Commerce (CIBC) was provided by Bradley Fedosoff, vice president, enterprise architecture, and Jose Ribau, senior vice president and chief data officer.

6. Sarah Halzack, "Amazon Will Open A Physical Grocery Store—and It Won't Require Going Through Checkout," *Washington Post*, December 5, 2016, www.washingtonpost.com/news/business/wp/2016/12/05/amazon-will-open-a-physical-grocery-store-and-it-wont-require-going-through-checkout.

7. MIT CISR 2015 CIO Digital Disruption Survey (413 participants). Top and bottom performers, respectively are top and bottom quartile on net profit margin, self-reported and adjusted for industry by subtracting the industry average.

8. BBVA, "Francisco González: "We Are Building the Best Digital Bank of the 21st Century," BBVA web page, March 13, 2015, www.bbva.com/en/francisco-gonzalez-we-are-building-the-best-digital-bank-of-the-21st-century.

9. The BBVA case study is based on many discussions with BBVA leaders; various BBVA documents; and BBVA.com, and is used with permission.

10. P. Weill and S. L. Woerner, "Is Your Company a Digital Leader or Digital Laggard?," *MIT CISR Briefing* 17, no. 3 (March 2017).

11. See BBVA, "BBVA, #1 in Mobile Banking in Europe," BBVA web page, May 17, 2017, www.bbva.com/en/bbva-1-mobile-banking-europe.

# Chapter 6

1. This chapter draws primarily from Weill and Woerner, "Digital Disruption (2014–2016)"; Weill and Woerner, "Boards (2014)"; and the following other study:

### Digital Workplace (2014-2016)

Our colleague Kristine Dery, along with Ina M. Sebastian and Nick van der Meulen, and with support from Jeanne W. Ross, led a study on the digital workplace, exploring how companies were redesigning work for the digital economy. They conducted interviews with sixty-three executives from twenty-seven large global companies and conducted a survey of 313 individuals. The survey measured the effectiveness of different facets of physical space, collaboration technologies, leadership styles, and organizational structures. Dery and her colleagues completed two cases studies, one on Deloitte Australia and one on DBS Bank in Singapore. In each case, they interviewed a number of senior executives.

2. K. Dery, I. M. Sebastian, and J. W. Ross, "The Digital Workplace Transforming Business: The Case of Deloitte Australia," *MIT CISR Briefing* 15, no. 8 (August 2015).

3. Unless noted, this sections draws on P. Weill and S. L. Woerner, "Becoming Better Prepared for Digital Disruption" *NACD Directorship* 2, no. 2 (March–April 2016); and P. Weill and S. L. Woerner, "Working with Your Board on Digital Disruption?," *MIT CISR Briefing* 15, no. 4 (April 2015). Our research on effective practices for boards on digital disruption drew insights from an online survey of eighty-three board members, nine lengthy phone interviews of directors, three in-depth case studies, and workshops conducted with more than twelve large company boards.

4. PwC, "Directors and IT: A user-friendly board guide for effective information technology oversight," abridged version, 2016, https://www.pwc.com/us/en/governance-insights-center/publications/assets/pwc-directors-and-it-abridged-gic.pdf.

5. The assessments of board activities the result of four recent polls of senior IT leaders during MIT CISR workshops in Cambridge, MA; Melbourne, Australia; and Warsaw, Poland. The participants evaluated the capabilities of their boards on each of the three roles on a scale of 1 to 9.

6. Emerson quote from MIT CISR interviews with company executives. Used with permission.

7. S. K. Sia, C. Soh and P. Weill, "How DBS Bank Pursued a Digital Business Strategy," *MIS Quarterly Executive* 15, no. 2 (June 2016); DBS website, www.dbs.com; K. Dery, I. M. Sebastian, and N. van der Meulen, "Building Business Value from the Digital Workplace," *MIT CISR Briefing* 16, no. 9 (September 2015): 4; S. K. Sia et al., "Rewiring the Enterprise for Digital Innovation: The Case of DBS Bank," publication ABCC-2015-004, Asian Business Case Centre, Nanyang Business School, Nanyang Technological University, Singapore, June 2, 2015.

8. S. Shome, "Disrupting growth markets," DBS presentation, November 17, 2017, https://www.dbs.com/investorday/presentations/Disrupting_Growth_Markets.pdf.

9. D. Gledhill, "Executing the digital strategy," DBS presentation, November 17, 2017, https://www.dbs.com/investorday/presentations/Executing_the_digital_strategy.pdf.

10. DBS, "DBS Named World's Most Digital Bank," press release, DBS, July 11, 2016.

11. K. Dery, I. M. Sebastian, and J. W. Ross, "The Digital Workplace Transforming Business: The Case of Deloitte Australia," *MIT CISR Briefing* 15, no. 8 (August 2015).

12. P. Weill, J. W. Ross, and S. L. Woerner, "Thriving with Digital Disruption: Five Propositions," *MIT CISR Briefing* 15, no. 7 (July 2015).

13. MIT CISR 2015 CIO Digitization Survey (413 participants). Top and bottom performers, respectively, are top quartile and bottom quartile on net profit margin, self-reported and adjusted for industry by subtracting the industry average.

14. P. Weill and S. L. Woerner, "How Other CxOs Think CIOs Should Spend Their Time," *MIT CISR Briefing* 10, no. 1 (January 2010). We found that the average CIO spends only 4.6 percent of time mentoring direct reports— insufficient time if the CIO plans to delegate responsibilities to them.

15. P. Weill and S. L. Woerner, "Top-Performing CIOs in the Digital Era," *MIT CISR Briefing* 16, no. 5 (May 2015).

16. Board questions and scores are from the MIT CISR 2014 Board Survey (83 participants). Top performers are the top quartile of net profit margin, adjusted for industry. Questions and scores for the other measures are from the MIT CISR 2015 Digital Disruption Survey (413 participants). Top performers are the top quartile of net profit margin, adjusted for industry. All differences are significant at $p < 0.05$. Scores for each question have been converted to a 1–10 scale.

# INDEX

# ACKNOWLEDGMENTS

We gratefully acknowledge the support of the approximately one hundred companies that are currently MIT CISR's patrons and sponsors; see cisr.mit.edu for the complete list.

These enterprises go beyond just informing and funding our research. They are an integral part of the MIT CISR community, where together we identify the big issues facing leaders, conduct research to understand best practices, and develop insights. These large companies not only provide data and case study examples, but also work with us on research projects. We conduct workshops at their offices to really dig into where they are and where they want to go. In the process, they help us understand, by their hard-earned experience and generosity in sharing, how to implement the major organizational changes needed to succeed.

We feel honored to work with such great leaders and so many terrific companies. Your passion, honesty, and clarity about the opportunities and threats that digital creates have helped us gain understanding. With that understanding, we use data and case studies to validate best practices and then share those practices with you. And in the process of iteration through many workshops, many presentations, and much writing, we refine the ideas and the messages. It's a marvelous community. A particularly big thank you to the managers who saw where our research could be better and told us. Those managers took the time to debate the issues with us and move our understanding forward.

A big thank you also to the anonymous reviewers and the many others who helped us on this manuscript. We would like to thank a few people specifically: Gary Scholten at Principal Financial, John Sviokla at PwC, Hervé Coureil and Jean-Pascal Tricoire at Schneider Electric, Francisco González and Carlos Torres Vila at BBVA, Shayne Elliott and Maile Carnegie and many others at ANZ Bank, Robert Samuel at Aetna, Jenny Banner at Schaad Companies and BB&T, and Patrick O'Rourke and many others at Microsoft. There are many other people we need to thank—we trust that you know who you are. Thank you for your input—you will see your insights in this book.

We thank all our fellow researchers at MIT CISR, who with their passion, talent, and camaraderie must be among the best research colleagues two researchers could ever have. Thank you, Jeanne Ross, Wanda Orlikowski, Barb Wixom, Kristine Dery, Nils Fonstad, Kate Moloney, Ina Sebastian, Nick van der Meulen, and Joe Peppard. Individually and together, they added encouragement, professionalism, collegiality, and insight—and lots of laughs. Also thanks to our research affiliates Martin Mocker, Cynthia (boo) Beath, Peter Hinssen, Peter Reynolds, Howard Rubin, and Tom Apel.

But it takes more than researchers to create a world-class research center. It takes great leadership and formidable administrators. First, a huge thank you to Leslie Owens, the executive director of MIT CISR. Leslie has that rare combination of vision, management skill, and empathy needed to lead an organization like ours. Chris Foglia, Cheryl Miller, and Amber Franey together provide extraordinary organization, content management, creativity, execution skills, and good humor. Thank you.

MIT CISR is a research center in the Sloan School of Management. We are very proud and privileged to work in such a rich and exciting research environment. We have benefited from the leadership, support, and encouragement of Dean David Schmittlein, Dean Ezra Zuckerman Sivan, and our IT group professorial colleagues Wanda Orlikowski, Stuart Madnick, Thomas Malone, Erik Brynjolfsson, and Sinan Aral. It's a huge pleasure to work with all of you.

We were pleased to work for the first time with Jeff Kehoe at Harvard Business Review Press (HBRP). Jeff's passion for creating great books, clarity of thinking and argument, and understanding of the marketplace have been a big contribution to this project. Thanks also to the wonderful Lucy McCauley, whose editing skills go way beyond making the text better to include collaborating with us so that we could say the right things more clearly and consistently. Thanks also to the great editorial group at HBRP.

Finally, a huge thank you to Dorothea Gray. Dorothea has made many contributions to the book, perhaps the most important of which is organizing us! Dorothea has conducted research, created diagrams, organized meetings and events, edited words, proofread, and many other jobs—all as a wonderful colleague. What makes Dorothea so good is not only her great skill but also her ability to work with people—from a CEO to the person who delivers packages—with great charm and respect, even under horrendous time pressures and with others around her in highly agitated states! Dorothea, we are grateful and really appreciate you.

## A Personal Note from Peter

I dedicate this book to the newest member of the small but global Weill family—Olivia Weill, who was born in 2016 and lives with her parents David Weill and Marta Salvador in Somers, Australia.

Olivia, it's for you and your generation that we do this research and try to help companies create more value for their customers and themselves. You deserve it. Thanks also to the rest of my Aussie family: Steven and Lois Weill, and Simon and Amy Weill for making it all worthwhile.

This book is the result of now more than ten years of partnership between Stephanie Woerner and me. Over those years, we have conducted many research projects on many different topics—all around the digitization of enterprises, financial performance, and the associated best practices. We have written many papers and created many presentations, and this is our first book together. Stephanie has many strengths. One strength I most admire is her ability to manage many research projects at the same time with conflicting demands and always delivering. Stephanie is a great colleague, and I really enjoy our many meetings debating the issues. A key element to our research is measuring the very difficult to measure, like ecosystems. I have met or worked with no one better at collecting data and measuring and analyzing these incredibly difficult constructs. This difficulty to measure is part of what creates value for the companies we work with. This is something they tell us again and again. Finally, Stephanie has another skill in huge quantities: resilience. Things don't always go according to plan in research and in life, but Stephanie always finds a way to deliver results and have fun while doing it.

A big hug and thank you to my wife, Margi Olson, PhD. You are the love of my life and my companion through it. You help make all this meaningful. Somehow, you manage to enjoy our crazy schedule, find the joy in almost everything, and be optimistic about most things—even the Red Sox! Your willingness to have, during our many walks and travels, endless conversations about digitization, large organizations, and how to change them is a gift. I look forward to many years of traveling the world together and trying to understand it better.

Without the help of three health professionals, I could not have done this work. To Dean Eliott, MD, at the Massachusetts Eye and Ear, thank you for restoring sight in my left eye—a huge gift. A big "Thanks, Mate" to the incomparable Tim Schleiger at 2Good Physiotherapy and Corrective Exercise. Tim helped me recover from hip surgery and now makes me closer to match fit. I was saddened by the recent passing of Dr. John Sarno, who worked for many years at NYU Medical School and helped me get rid of debilitating back pain. John was an unheralded pioneer in understanding the mind-body connection, and I hope he now receives the credit he always deserved.

To my mother, Hilde Bette Weill, and my father, Hans "Jonny" Weill, thank you. Although no longer with us physically, you remain in my heart. Thanks for your love, generous spirit, good genes, and great values.

## A Personal Note from Stephanie

First, I thank Peter for our research partnership. Peter is a creative, exacting researcher, and I have learned a lot from him. He is often on the road, talking to executives about the challenges of building successful enterprises in the digital economy. He is a superb synthesizer of those conversations and always returns to the office with new ideas for research projects, often on topics that have been studied infrequently, if at all. Our brainstorming sessions are a delight—all ideas about how to study a topic are fair game. I can't wait to see what issues we tackle in the next ten years.

My children, Max, Jack, and Zoe, and my daughter-in-law, Chris, keep me grounded and make my life rich. Watching my children and their friends support each other and listening to them struggle with how to make the world a better, more accepting place makes me optimistic about the future.

My parents, Charles and Judith Woerner, have always given me unconditional love. They've backed me up and encouraged me to take risks. My in-laws, John and Pricilla Chase, are terrific. I can't count the number of times they've stepped in and taken care of their grandchildren so I could go on work trips or spend time with my husband. My siblings, Charlie, Susan, Mary, Teresa, and Ruth, are dear to me. I treasure the times we spend together—let's do it more often.

Tina Underwood has been my best friend since graduate school. We've shared children problems and successes, recipes, quilting techniques, and our struggles to build careers while raising families—our phone calls are a highlight of my week. Susan Krusell, whom I first met at CISR, is one of the connectors in this world, and she has introduced me to so many interesting people. Pete Reynolds, Anne Quaadgras, and Martin Mocker, all formerly at MIT CISR, have been probing questioners and supportive colleagues. Pamela Enders has been an encouraging coach, helping me grow and branch out. I especially want to thank Wanda Orlikowski for hiring me to be a project manager and researcher on a National Science Foundation grant in 2000, giving me an entrée into the fascinating world that I work on now.

I dedicate this book to my husband, David Chase. Thank you, David, for all your love, support, and encouragement over the years. Raising a family and working full-time is a challenge, and David has been a partner through all the struggles and joys. He's a good editor (all those years of Latin study have been good for something), an engaged listener, and great fun. I'm looking forward to more adventures.

# ABOUT THE AUTHORS

**PETER D. WEILL**, BE, MBA, MPhil, PhD, is the Chairman of MIT CISR at the Sloan School of Management, which studies and works with companies on how to transform for success in the digital era. MIT CISR has approximately one hundred company members globally who use, debate, support, and participate in the research. Peter's work centers on the role, value, and governance of digitization in enterprises and their ecosystems. Ziff Davis recognized Peter as number twenty-four of "The Top 100 Most Influential People in IT" and the highest-ranked academic. This is Peter's sixth book for Harvard Business Review Press.

**STEPHANIE L. WOERNER**, MBA, MA, PhD, is a research scientist at MIT CISR. Her research centers on how companies manage organizational change caused by the digitization of the economy. She has a passion for measuring hard-to-assess digital factors such as connectivity and customer experience and linking them to firm performance. Stephanie earned her PhD in organizational behavior at the Stanford University Graduate School of Business.